# Cambridge Elements

Elements in Beckett Studies
edited by
Dirk Van Hulle
*University of Oxford*
Mark Nixon
*University of Reading*

# SUZANNE DUMESNIL, SUZANNE BECKETT

Emilie Morin
*University of York*

Shaftesbury Road, Cambridge CB2 8EA, United Kingdom

One Liberty Plaza, 20th Floor, New York, NY 10006, USA

477 Williamstown Road, Port Melbourne, VIC 3207, Australia

314–321, 3rd Floor, Plot 3, Splendor Forum, Jasola District Centre, New Delhi – 110025, India

103 Penang Road, #05–06/07, Visioncrest Commercial, Singapore 238467

Cambridge University Press is part of Cambridge University Press & Assessment, a department of the University of Cambridge.

We share the University's mission to contribute to society through the pursuit of education, learning and research at the highest international levels of excellence.

www.cambridge.org
Information on this title: www.cambridge.org/9781009585576

DOI: 10.1017/9781009585545

© Emilie Morin 2025

This publication is in copyright. Subject to statutory exception and to the provisions of relevant collective licensing agreements, no reproduction of any part may take place without the written permission of Cambridge University Press & Assessment.

When citing this work, please include a reference to the DOI 10.1017/9781009585545

First published 2025

*A catalogue record for this publication is available from the British Library*

ISBN 978-1-009-58557-6 Hardback
ISBN 978-1-009-58556-9 Paperback
ISSN 2632-0746 (online)
ISSN 2632-0738 (print)

Cambridge University Press & Assessment has no responsibility for the persistence or accuracy of URLs for external or third-party internet websites referred to in this publication and does not guarantee that any content on such websites is, or will remain, accurate or appropriate.

For EU product safety concerns, contact us at Calle de José Abascal, 56, 1°, 28003 Madrid, Spain, or email eugpsr@cambridge.org

# Suzanne Dumesnil, Suzanne Beckett

Elements in Beckett Studies

DOI: 10.1017/9781009585545
First published online: July 2025

Emilie Morin
*University of York*
Author for correspondence: Emilie Morin, emilie.morin@york.ac.uk

**Abstract:** Little has been written about Suzanne Beckett, née Déchevaux-Dumesnil (1900–89). As Samuel Beckett's lifelong companion, she found herself in a peculiar quandary, owing to the amounts of support required by Beckett's unease with success and with the business of writing, and owing to her deep awareness of the damage that fame can cause to everyday life, friendships and freedom. This Element offers the first full portrait of this elusive figure. It contextualises the texts she wrote under the name Suzanne Dumesnil, emphasises the significance of her artistic and literary accomplishments, and discusses her steady labour, her uncompromising discretion and her profound reluctance to ever become a public figure as Beckett's wife.

This Element has a video abstract: www.cambridge.org/EIBS_Morin_abstract

**Keywords:** Suzanne Beckett, née Déchevaux-Dumesnil (1900–89), Samuel Beckett, modernist wives, fame, biography

© Emilie Morin 2025

ISBNs: 9781009585576 (HB), 9781009585569 (PB), 9781009585545 (OC)
ISSNs: 2632-0746 (online), 2632-0738 (print)

# Contents

1 Introduction: Silent Companion    1

2 Argenteuil, Tunis, Paris (1900–38)    11

3 Suzanne after Beckett, from 1938 to the War's Aftermath    25

4 The Writings of Suzanne Dumesnil    31

5 The Quiet Work of Suzanne Beckett    47

6 Portraits in Different Shades    53

7 Conclusion    63

   References    66

# 1 Introduction: Silent Companion

The state of affairs around Suzanne Beckett is unusual. She believed in Samuel Beckett's talent more than anyone and their relationship lasted over fifty years, coinciding with Beckett's whole career as a French-language author. Yet, in the vast biographical literature on Beckett, Suzanne recedes as soon as she appears, into a mysterious world of piano playing, silence and refusal. Information about her was exceedingly scarce until recently. One cannot help but notice the contrast with other research fields: there are no mysteries around the work that Nora Joyce, George Yeats or Véra Nabokov, for example, did to keep their husbands afloat. Suzanne shunned the limelight more keenly than others; evidently, she was profoundly wary of the damage that fame can inflict. Beckett felt that her relation to fame was even more ambivalent than his (JEK/A/7/47; JEK/A/7/61; JEK/A/7/69). When she sought recognition, it was as an author in her own right – as Suzanne Dumesnil – but always discreetly, and she came to realise that the shadow cast by Beckett's writing would never disappear. 'Tu comprends, pour eux, je suis "la Beckett"' ('You see, to them, "la Beckett" is who I am'), she once confided (AMC), in a concise articulation of what became a painful problem as Beckett's success grew.[1] This Element traces her unusual life and offers a portrait that foregrounds her creativity and disregard of conventions. Throughout, I refer to my subject as Suzanne, in keeping with established custom in biographies of major writers and their wives – not least because she became Suzanne Beckett in her early sixties and lived most of her life under her maiden name, Déchevaux-Dumesnil.

In literary history, Suzanne has gone down as a woman of action rather than words – unfailingly brave, quick-thinking and wise in emergencies. We can infer, from James Knowlson especially, that she saved Beckett's life several times during the Second World War; she understood how to act when she was arrested and interrogated and when they needed to hide and escape. She showed great lucidity, too, when she improvised herself as Beckett's agent in 1949 and thereafter, and has been widely acknowledged as the person who made his career possible thanks to her determination to preserve the environment he needed to write. 'I owe everything to Suzanne', Beckett said to Knowlson after her death (Knowlson, 1996, 376). 'I kept out of the way', he recalled, sketching a portrait of Suzanne wandering the streets with his typescripts, courting Parisian publishers, theatre directors and concierges. In hindsight, his turn away from the promise of a life of plenty with Peggy Guggenheim to

---

[1] My interviewees are designated as AMC (Anne-Marie Colombard), AD (Alexandre Dandelot), MG (Marthe Gautier), CS (Claude Salzman) and MTW (Michèle Tholozan-Warluzel). They are introduced further on. Translations from French are mine unless otherwise indicated.

embrace a modest life with Suzanne shaped everything else. With this relationship, which opened up another side of France previously closed to him as a foreigner, the most atypical and unpredictable period of his existence began. Shortly after Suzanne settled with him on Rue des Favorites in 1940, they fled Paris on an epic journey to Vichy, then Arcachon. After the *exode* they returned to their small flat, to a life punctuated by scarcity of all things and underground Resistance work. In 1942, when the Gloria SMH cell was denounced to the Gestapo, they relied on Communist friends of Suzanne's who were organised and experienced, and found refuge in Roussillon through other friends of Suzanne's (Knowlson and Knowlson, 2006, 80, 85). They became used to living with very little and got through the hard times that followed together. Each decade brought new difficulties. But the pact between them – if it can be called thus – endured. When Suzanne died on 17 July 1989, at the age of eighty-nine, Beckett outlived her by five months. They rest in the same grave in Montparnasse Cemetery.

Beckett's life has been closely scrutinised, with three major biographies, over a dozen satellite biographies in French and in English, countless biographical derivatives in other formats, and numerous memoirs and essays detailing encounters, friendships and collaborations. This literature is extremely diverse, except when it comes to Suzanne, who remains confined to the background – at best discreet, mostly unaccommodating, often absent, largely silent and widely remembered for greeting Beckett's Nobel Prize as a 'catastrophe'. Her practical support and sense of initiative are acknowledged, but her intellect and talent are rarely mentioned. Her caregiving, too, stays in the shadows, and she is commonly presented as someone Beckett grew tired of quickly. Owing to a throwaway comment Beckett made in rehearsal (Bair, 1978, 483), she is often assimilated to the forlorn characters of *Waiting for Godot* and *Endgame*. They always lived together, but the assumption that the life they shared was not authentic enough looms large (see Bair, 1978, 357–8, 478, 508–9, 533 and later derivative accounts). At worst, her name acts as a prompt to mention Beckett's affairs (Dukes, 2001, 63). The layout of their home on Boulevard Saint-Jacques, which had two entrances, has been presented as evidence of irremediable estrangement (e.g. Calder, 2001, 327–8; Rosset, 2016, 125), although such a layout is not unusual in mid-twentieth-century Parisian flats. Ostensibly, nothing is known of their intimate life – everything is speculation – yet assumptions have routinely been made about the degree of intimacy between them, with conclusions drawn accordingly. Over time, Barbara Bray – Beckett's long-term mistress, who had a rich career at the BBC and as a literary translator (see Sardin, 2024b) – has received far more generous and rational treatment.

It is no accident, then, that James Marsh's 2023 film biopic *Dance First* should choose to introduce her as 'Suzanne from the tennis' and chart her transformation from a young girl with a good dress sense but without much to say into Beckett's sullen cook and secretary, who pleads in hesitant English, wears dowdy clothes and lacks everything the vivacious and stylish Bray brings (*Dance First*, 2023). In the biographical literature, the more derivative the account is, the more caricatural and spiteful its treatment of Suzanne becomes (Huston, 2004, 87–8; Schneiderman, 1988, 165–6; Strathern, 2005, 86). What we can discern in such implausible portraits is not so much a distorted relation to facts and context but the commercial imperative that underpins surprisingly large amounts of anecdotal and biographical writing about Beckett. When the story needs to sell, it is more tempting to speak of distance, separation and solitude and to romanticise affairs than to try to render the humdrum realities of a long relationship. The wider picture, of course, tells us that authors' wives who have attracted biographical attention are the exception rather than the norm. Always there, but taken for granted; crucial, but mostly invisible: this tends to be the fate of those who laboured for the success of another. The glamour of fame and enduring ideas about writerly genius offer easier narrative material, more compelling stories than support relentlessly given, drafts read, diaries managed, domestic chores completed, nearest and dearest cared for.

Sources, and not simply focus, have posed challenges: indeed, the quantity, quality and reliability of the information used to apprehend Suzanne's personality and life have varied enormously. What makes *Damned to Fame: The Life of Samuel Beckett* so important in this context is that it is the only work that sketches out Suzanne's character and interests and uses reliable sources (Knowlson, 1996, 296, 473–4). Previously, much was built on hearsay and imagination. Deirdre Bair's sensationalist biography, known for its denigratory treatment of Suzanne, has left a long shadow, discernible not simply in popular books but also in scholarly biographies that tried to eschew anything questionable or distorted and were left with very few facts about Suzanne (Brater, 1989, 38, 42, 59; Gordon, 1996, 4, 60, 133). Anthony Cronin's *Samuel Beckett: The Last Modernist* seems broadly sympathetic, but the passages mentioning Suzanne extrapolate from Bair's biography, were borrowed from Knowlson's proofs (Cronin, [1996] 1997, 294; Knowlson, 1996, 296; see also Arnold, 1999) or come across as pure speculation, with unsupported facts and narration disguised as evidence of proximity. Over time, Knowlson's more grounded portrait has taken precedence, as shown in biographical accounts by David Pattie (2000), Nathalie Léger (2006) and Andrew Gibson (2010) which make brief but explicit attempts to let Suzanne in. Gibson, building on Knowlson's evocation of Suzanne's 'decisive left-wing opinions' (Knowlson, 1996, 296), introduces her as 'an interesting woman, a *gauchiste* with Communist friends and a social conscience' and 'the most important woman in Beckett's later life' (Gibson, 2010, 97). Overall, however, the volume of writing dedicated to Suzanne is extremely small, often repetitive, and focuses on determining moments when her presence proved useful: Beckett's stabbing, the war, the search for publishers and theatres, the Nobel Prize. There is one exception: an impressionistic portrait by Bettina Jonic that celebrates a 'handsome, loyal and courageously bold' woman who 'did the leg work' tenaciously and gracefully, shouldered 'The burden of [Beckett's] perpetual low keyed intense moods', refused to put up with people she held in low esteem and stayed true to her principles (Jonic, 2010).

The problem of Suzanne's invisibility has left odd traces. Take her physical appearance: the photographs show a tall, blonde, slender woman who dressed elegantly and formally, and looked athletic all her life including in her late seventies (Banier, 2009; Tholozan-Warluzel, 2024). Yet Martin Esslin described her as 'a stumpy little woman' (Knowlson, 2006, 147) and Herbert Blau as a nondescript woman with 'reddish hair, ill-fitting suit' (Blau, 2000, 1). The journalist Francis Evers assumed that she was Beckett's 'maid or home help' because she kept silent and Beckett called her Suzanne (Cronin, [1996] 1997, 508). Her maiden name, Déchevaux-Dumesnil, has been persistently misspelt as Deschevaux-Dumesnil in Beckett scholarship, although it is engraved above Beckett's name on their tombstone – a grave visited by so many, with photographs disseminated far and wide – and although correct spellings were in circulation from 1969 onwards, in directories including *The Blue Book* and Cleveland Amory and Earl Blackwell's *Celebrity Register*. Her formation as a pianist has been widely acknowledged, but vaguely and in passing. Her writing has proved a contentious matter, with 'F–', 'Les Joues rouges' and other 'Petit Sot' poems widely attributed to Beckett, which has turned the recent emergence of typescripts unambiguously signed Suzanne Dumesnil into an important moment of reckoning for Beckett studies. Previously, just one archival document had been attributed to her: an undated piece of music paper catalogued at the Harry Ransom Center as 'J'aurai seize ans aux fleurs nouvelles …', featuring three lines from a song (MS 19.14). Suzanne is not the author; the manuscript only points to her great musical memory. The lyrics and melody are from Etienne Singla and C. Henri's 'J'aurai seize ans', a song originally published in G clef (Henri and Singla, 1869), converted to C clef in Suzanne's hand. The lyrics – wistful, richly evocative yet economical – are about the ambivalent transformation from youth to adulthood and, indirectly, about each beginning carrying its own ending. As with much involving Suzanne, we can only speculate about the discussions that surrounded this score, its existence hinting at decades of conversations, thoughts and ideas recorded in a most fragmentary form.

Of course, I am not the first to point to Suzanne's occultation. In recent musings on insomniac and restless sleepers – a category to which Beckett belonged (JEK/A/7/8) – the novelist Marie Darrieussecq evokes a writing tradition that transforms women into mere shadows in Parisian intellectual and artistic history: 'Beckett and Cioran are always presented as two loners, but their wives, Suzanne Déchevaux-Dumesnil and Simone Boué, were with them throughout their lives. As was the case with their friend Giacometti and his wife, Annette Arm' (Darrieussecq, 2023, 122–3). Within Beckett studies, the debate around Suzanne has largely unfolded in book reviews, of Bair's biography especially: Angela Moorjani denounced its hostility towards Suzanne and other women (Moorjani, 1978, 1114); Richard Ellmann objected to its presentation of gossip from 'chatterbox friends' as the truth (Ellmann, 1978, 4); Calvin Israel pointed to a 'savage delimiting portrait' informed by 'the resentful remarks of Peggy Guggenheim' and 'the envy, misunderstanding, and gossip of others who, in the main, are not identified' (Israel, 1979, 82–3). Before *Damned to Fame* appeared, Robert Pinget observed that Suzanne had been 'mistreated by some of Beckett's biographers' and yearned for greater accuracy (Renouard, 1993, 241–2). Only once has someone argued for dedicated biographical work: in a review of *Damned to Fame*, William Hutchings called for 'a separate biography of Suzanne comparable to Brenda Maddox's volume on Nora Joyce', arguing that '[Suzanne] remains entirely too silent a figure in this biography – and is now more fascinating than ever' (Hutchings, 1997, 598). Later, reviewing James and Elizabeth Knowlson's *Beckett Remembering/Remembering Beckett*, Beverley Curran noted the rarity of references to Suzanne and wished to see her featured among the interviewees (Curran, 2006, 141).

Unfortunately, this longing for something closer to life, while sincere and compelling, is out of step with what could ever be gathered. Although fleeting moments in Beckett's life are narrated from Suzanne's perspective in the major biographies, and although some of Bair's reviewers suggested personal knowledge of Suzanne's life, Suzanne did not meet any of Beckett's biographers, did not speak to critics interested in Beckett's work, communicated with very few of Beckett's anglophone collaborators and always thought of herself as an independent person who was not accountable to Beckett's friends or to anyone writing about him. In formal gatherings she could be profoundly ill at ease (JEK/A/7/47). 'I have been asked over the years, again and again, didn't I find her bizarre', Jonic noted in 1999 (Jonic, 2010). She never fitted in Parisian dinner parties – a world where shyness and unusual taste were not forgiven and women's garments could be looked at closely (JEK/A/7/56). The silence around her, with its strong flavour of disapproval, has much to do with her refusal to conform.

In the Beckett archives, too, there is a void. Of course, much of life happens without leaving a trace and very little ends up in archival boxes. But the contrast between the abundant records of Beckett's thoughts and whereabouts (nearly 10,000 of his letters have been preserved in archives across Europe and North America) and the scant traces of Suzanne is spectacular. The contrast between Suzanne's near-absence and the abundant documentation of Beckett's relationship with Bray is just as striking. In Beckett's available papers, the most detailed messages in Suzanne's hand are the few letters to Jérôme Lindon and Roger Blin held at the IMEC (Institut Mémoires de l'édition contemporaine). Elsewhere, in the catalogues of antiquarian book dealers, some very occasional letters and postcards from Suzanne to Monique Haas, Edith Fournier and Georges Adet's wife have appeared, but there is nothing in them that is not already evident elsewhere. Letters addressed to Suzanne no longer exist. Like Beckett, she would destroy her correspondence – immediately, if the message came from Beckett (MG; JEK/A/7/28). She was always an economical writer (even when discussing vital matters such as care for her mother, her postcards were brief) and she preferred communicating by phone. Especially after the 1950s, the few photographs of her that remain are identity photographs or were taken without her permission. She never owned a camera (JEK/A/7/28) and did not want relatives to photograph her after a certain age (Tholozan-Warluzel, 2024, 155). Gathering information about her was probably the most arduous task that Knowlson faced as Beckett's authorised biographer, not least because Suzanne's most loyal friends remained guarded in interviews. At best, the interviewees who knew Suzanne well gave elliptic or awkward answers to Knowlson's questions. At worst, those less acquainted with Suzanne revelled in the power that being interviewed gave them over this woman they barely knew and engaged in ill-intentioned gossip. The paucity of information reflects a wider truth: Suzanne did not speak much in most circumstances, and her formidable personality meant that even those close to her were reluctant to ask questions. She confided in others only when she felt like it and rarely talked about the past; when she did, it was in vague terms (AMC; MTW).

From Beckett's correspondence little surfaces; Suzanne is mentioned less and less over time. It can often seem as though she is not there at all in postcards and letters he sent during their long holidays together, even when the recipient is not Bray, with whom Beckett started a relationship in the late 1950s. Elsewhere, in biographical sketches heavily based on conversations with Beckett, Suzanne features as an unnamed wife (Janvier, 1969, 16), is entirely absent (Harvey,

1970) or is mentioned as the person who acts as Beckett's secretary, runs errands (Juliet, 1999, 13, 45) and buys clothes (Bernold, 1992, 101). Conversational traits also had an impact: indeed, Beckett's default tendency was to speak in the first-person singular – a habit that struck Suzanne's friend Michèle Meunier because Suzanne mostly spoke in the plural, using *nous* or *on* (JEK/A/7/59). High levels of secrecy were the norm around Beckett and biographically inclined French critics struggled especially hard. Pierre Mélèse could not reach Beckett and collected testimonies from collaborators instead (Mélèse, 1966, 136). Guy Croussy was instructed by Lindon to look for answers in Beckett's work, and Gérard Durozoi was not granted an interview either (Lindon to Croussy, 10 July 1969; Lindon to Durozoi, 5 October 1970, IMEC). Alfred Simon later suggested, in a stand-off with Lindon over his tasteless and improbable portrayal of the Becketts at the end of their lives, that factual accuracy was impossible because nobody was willing to share information (Lindon and Simon, 1992, 176).

That there was an agreement to keep Suzanne out of the picture is evident from successive first-hand sources presenting her as a mystery. 'As usual, though I asked, he wouldn't talk much of Suzanne', Herbert Blau observed in an account of meeting Beckett in 1959 (Blau, 2000, 20). Jay Levy never saw her in the flat on Boulevard Saint-Jacques; he only heard her in the kitchen, sometime in 1961: 'I would in later sessions ask to meet her, but never did' (Levy, 1998, 198). This was also Knowlson's experience: during the 1970s, he sometimes heard Suzanne in the flat but neither met nor saw her (JEK/A/7/24). John Fletcher discovered over two years after first meeting Beckett, also in the flat, that Suzanne Dumesnil was his wife, from notes Beckett sent him about his translations (10 September 1963, HRHRC; Fletcher, 2016, 30). Bair remembered Beckett's reluctance to speak about Suzanne over forty years after their conversations: 'Although [Beckett] introduced her name easily into almost every conversation, and he always gave her credit for the struggles she endured to bring his work to publication, her name invariably brought on that deep red blush, a prelude to a quick flash of anger, so I took care to change the subject quickly when these occasions arose' (Bair, 2020, 78–9). With Knowlson, too, Suzanne was a firmly controlled topic: when work on the biography began, Beckett confided that there were just two things he wanted to say about Suzanne – that his debt to her was beyond measure, and that she hated success even more than he did (JEK/A/7/47; JEK/A/7/61; JEK/A/7/69).

Beckett let his guard down on one occasion. In 1983, in a conversation with Rosette Lamont, he acknowledged Suzanne as the person for whom he returned to a country at war, his Resistance comrade, his liaison with the theatre world and the influence behind his understanding of dramaturgy:

> In 1939, having heard Chamberlain's announcement of the war on the radio, I did everything in my power to return to France. I wanted to join Suzanne, who was not yet my wife at the time. Above all I did not wish to remain safely blocked in Ireland. When I reached Dover, [...] I wept, implored, begged, and they allowed me to leave. During the Occupation, Suzanne and I worked in the Resistance. Our group was denounced by a traitor in our midst in '42. Most of my comrades were arrested. [...] Suzanne and I were lucky. We had received warning in time and sought refuge in the apartment of a Communist friend of ours in Paris [...]. I knew almost nothing about dramaturgy when I became a playwright, and since I never went to the theater, I had to rely on Suzanne for information. It was she who told me about Blin, and who took my manuscripts around. (Lamont, 1995, 34)

This sense that the partnership was of utmost significance and that love ran deep is echoed elsewhere. In a moving letter to Susan Manning after his mother's death, Beckett hoped that he and Suzanne would never have to be apart again (10 September 1950, HRHRC). In later conversations, Levy noticed how Beckett's face lit up whenever he spoke about Suzanne (Levy, 1998, 201). The photos François-Marie Banier took in Tangier in 1978 show a couple in harmony, perfectly synchronised (Banier, 2009). Likewise, the elderly couple Didier Anzieu saw in the Bois de Vincennes, probably ten years later, seemed an indestructible unit (Anzieu, 1992, 15). The resemblances between them were so striking, Hermine Karagheuz noted, that Suzanne could come across as a heightened version of Beckett himself (JEK/A/7/42). Most biographical sources, however, speak of habit, tired solidarity, co-dependency, resentment and irritation. The only publication to evoke love is Richard Seaver's memoir, which acknowledges in a footnote '[Beckett's] beloved Suzanne, who had personally traipsed around Paris for years with copies of *Molloy* and *Malone* under her arm, looking in vain for a publisher' (Seaver, 2011, 154).

Because so little of Suzanne's own writing could be discussed until recently, and because she did enormous amounts of work to support Beckett's career, the void around her should be grasped in all its complexity, along with the difficulties that arise when trying to recreate a sense of someone despite many layers of absence. These are questions to which a new tradition of feminist biography – which has emerged strongly in France, in relation to artistic milieux that overlapped with those of the Becketts – has brought some answers, by explicitly working its way out of absences, scrutinising fragments and anecdotes, and mapping out friendships, relationships and networks. In *Villa Chagrin*, Marie Cosnay uses the remnants of a disappeared archive and sporadic diary-keeping to recreate the tireless dedication with which Marthe Kuntz-Arnaud (herself a writer) enabled Bram Van Velde to paint in the midst of adversity (Cosnay, 2006). In *Sylvia Bataille*, Angie David narrates the life of Sylvia Maklès-Bataille-Lacan, a renowned film actress married to Georges Bataille, then Jacques Lacan, who has been infrequently mentioned in their biographies. Maklès, like Suzanne, destroyed most of her correspondence (David, 2013, 283–4). David turns to Maklès's films, memories of relatives and scholarship on French surrealism to trace her itinerary as a prolific working artist, upon whom Bataille relied to fund his lifestyle and excesses, until her marriage to Lacan, when her career came to a sharp halt. In *Gabriële*, Anne and Claire Berest describe how their ancestor Francis Picabia mined his wife's artistic and intellectual resources. Their biography, too, is based on a void: by the time Gabriële Buffet-Picabia died, all belongings and papers had been stolen or had vanished from her flat (Berest and Berest, 2017, 320–1).

Here too – in a different way – I work with discontinuities, traces and crevices and pay close attention to friendships and family recollections. I push Beckett to the margins to make space for other narratives – like Pascale Sardin, who renders Beckett as the 'minor figure' and Bray as the 'major figure' in her biography of Bray (Sardin, 2024a, 183). The thick silence around Suzanne had always intrigued me but, like other Beckett scholars, I couldn't find any information with which to break it. What allowed me to do this work in the first place is a biographical essay – now published in English translation – that Suzanne's great-niece Michèle Tholozan-Warluzel sent me, following a discussion of fragmentary correspondence in the *Watt* notebooks, and her generous offer to show me the family photographs, letters and postcards preserved by her great-grandmother, Jeanne Déchevaux-Dumesnil, and her grandmother Andrée, Suzanne's sister. My other first-hand sources are the interviews I conducted with Michèle Tholozan-Warluzel, Anne-Marie Colombard (another of Suzanne's great-nieces, who was close to her), Claude Salzman (son of Suzanne's friend Ruth Stern-Salzman) and the late Marthe Gautier (one of Suzanne's closest friends in later life), and a biographical essay that Manolo Fandos wrote in response to my research. Other crucial insights were assembled from Suzanne's writings, from traces of her input in the Beckett archives, from James Knowlson's archived interviews for *Damned to Fame*, which date from the late 1980s and the early 1990s, and from manuscripts, typescripts, books and letters from the Beckett Digital Manuscript Project and physical archives. Readers should remain keenly aware that, in keeping with the dominant custom in Beckett studies over the past fifteen years, I use paraphrase for unpublished materials by the Becketts – not out of personal choice but because current licensing and copyright arrangements for electronic publishing formats make direct citation extremely difficult.

From this peculiar mass of materials a consistent picture emerges, of someone who led her life as she wanted, as much as she possibly could. What defines Suzanne's life is not simply that she gravitated towards atypical profiles and personalities but that she acted in ways that grated against expectations, against norms, in ways that were specific to her and her environment. Alberto Chiarini's memories of May 1968 illustrate well what I mean by this. Suzanne, then sixty-eight, was fascinated by the discussions taking place: Chiarini, her close friend, recalled that they would go nearly every evening to the Odéon-Théâtre de France, then occupied by the student movement, to listen to the debates hosted there (JEK/A/7/19). President De Gaulle's response – he refused to step down, dissolved the National Assembly and gave a speech associating the revolts with totalitarian Communism – came as an enormous shock to Suzanne (JEK/A/7/19). Beckett also had deep sympathy for the student revolt (AMC), but his experience of 1968 was markedly different. When the *évènements* erupted, Beckett, then unwell, had been dedicating his energy to helping André Malraux – a key symbol of Gaullist France as Minister of Culture and the person who dismissed Jean-Louis Barrault as director of the Odéon soon after – organise the Henri Hayden exhibition at the Musée National d'Art Moderne (JEK/A/7/33).

There is something poignant about Suzanne's enthusiasm, given how debates about women's rights gained prevalence with the cultural revolution of 1968. Most advances towards gender equality in France happened too late for her to benefit directly. When she was young, it was unthinkable to attempt the baccalaureate; by the time French women were allowed to take the baccalaureate on a par with men, she was twenty-four and had probably completed her studies at the Ecole Normale de Musique. She was thirty-eight when portions of the Napoleonic Code depriving married women of most basic rights and freedoms were repealed with visible public impact. She was forty-four when she gained the right to vote. In 1961, when she married Beckett in Folkestone, England, French matrimonial law still forbade married women from looking after their own interests: they could not open a bank account or exercise a profession without their husbands' permission, for example. When larger swathes of matrimonial law inherited from the Napoleonic Code were repealed, giving married women fuller ownership over their own affairs, Suzanne was sixty-five. If she looked upon the institution of marriage with contempt and remained a fierce advocate of *l'union libre* or common law partnership (Tholozan-Warluzel, 2024, 151), this was also because she understood the degree to which marriage meant deprivation of rights, not simply loss of independence. By the time use of the contraceptive pill became legal in France, Suzanne was sixty-seven; by the time abortion became legal, she was seventy-five. These are blunt examples, but they have the merit of bringing into the frame wider social contexts and generational concerns that might otherwise recede from sight.

The structure of this Element is partly chronological and partly thematic, as befits a life and work from which only fragments remain. When there are only residues to work with, writing a 'normal' biography is impossible. Sections 2 and 3 are biographical: I trace Suzanne's artistic education, interests and friendships during her youth and adulthood, then her life from 1938 – when her relationship with Beckett begins – to the war's aftermath. Section 4 surveys what currently survives of the texts she authored as Suzanne Dumesnil between the mid-1930s and the late 1960s, tracing difficult entanglements of publication and authorship, and moving between the world of publishing to the personal world of writing into which she retreated from the early 1950s onwards. Section 5 considers Suzanne's informal work for Beckett and highlights her contributions to the genesis of his French texts and the life of his plays in performance. Section 6 discusses the perspectives on Suzanne's personality offered by her friends and relatives, noting their sharp contrast with memoirs focused on Beckett. Attempting to rethink Suzanne's place in the well-charted narrative of Beckett's life is certainly a sobering experience, but also one that sheds salutary light on persistent myths – including the myth of the genius who matures alone from one success to another.

## 2 Argenteuil, Tunis, Paris (1900–38)

Suzanne's background has been a sticking point in biographies of Beckett. It has been asserted that she came from Troyes (Bair, 1978, 280; Cronin, [1996] 1997, 294) and Châlons (Léger, 2006, 88), but she was born in Argenteuil, a town northwest of Paris beyond Saint-Denis and Nanterre, partly delimited by the Seine river. In 1900, the year of her birth, Argenteuil was a rapidly growing industrial town with a large working-class population and a strong Communist presence. On her mother's side ran a line of shopkeepers from Argenteuil (Tholozan, n.d.); her grandfather Joseph Fourniols – who was working as a tailor and living with her parents on her birth date, 7 January 1900 – had worked in successive clothes shops. He specialised in workers' garments, as suggested by a childhood photograph of Suzanne's mother, Jeanne, in front of a shop called 'L'Incroyable Bon Marché' recovered by Jean-Pierre Tholozan as part of his genealogical research on his family.[2] Suzanne's father Paul worked as a shop employee when she was a baby. His own father had been a telegraphist in Cherbourg. The hyphenated family name, Déchevaux-Dumesnil, was the creation of an enterprising ancestor who went from serving the French Revolution to

---

[2] A pun referring to incredible bargains and to Le Bon Marché, the luxury department store in Paris.

aspiring for a higher social status, and who added his grandmother's name, Mesnil, to his own, Déchevaux, thus transmitting a double-barrel name suggestive of fallen nobility to his descendants (Tholozan, n.d.). Suzanne, for her part, took a cordial dislike to 'Déchevaux': Dumesnil is the surname she used for her sister and for herself – as an author, with her friends and when representing Beckett.[3]

In a moving memoir, Michèle Tholozan-Warluzel relates what is known of Suzanne's childhood and youth (Tholozan-Warluzel, 2024). Paul Déchevaux-Dumesnil's health quickly became a matter of concern. In 1902, the family moved to Tunis, in search of a warmer, dryer climate. Suzanne and her sister Andrée were two and five, respectively. Tunis brought new opportunities and upward mobility: the family lived in a small villa and Paul worked as an *agent de fabrique*, a sales representative, probably in import-export. Jeanne took to wearing lighter, looser-fitting clothes and Paul became fond of Tunisian garments, the surviving family photographs show. As for Suzanne, she went through the rites of passage in good society, with music lessons, a conventional Catholic education and a first communion in Tunis Cathedral. Her talent for the piano became quickly evident and the family resources were invested into nurturing it. From Suzanne's later confidences to Edith Fournier, we can infer that she was interested in the instrument, not the symbol of feminine achievement: when she earned a diploma she secretly tore it to pieces and said nothing. Her mother found out when the piano teacher congratulated her on her daughter's success (JEK/A/7/27).

Family life was harmonious, but Suzanne and Andrée struggled with their mother's temperament. Jeanne, while outwardly gentle, could be difficult to please and liked to have her own way (MTW; AMC). Paul was easier company – probably 'more eccentric, more demonstrative, more affectionate even' (Tholozan-Warluzel, 2024, 138). Jeanne's strict, conventional outlook spurred her daughters to develop a strong dislike of social and religious norms from a young age (138). It seems that Suzanne became more rebellious as she entered adulthood; at the end of her life, she recalled that her first love affair had been with a Tunisian man (JEK/A/7/27). This would have been anathema even in the most liberal French families of Tunis, where 'Europeans' and 'Arabs' did not mix easily or casually, and marriage had to be firmly on the cards (marriages with Tunisians remained the preserve of the large Italian population; Memmi, 1985, 43). The novella Suzanne completed in 1947, 'Françoise', tells a poignant story involving social taboos and racial shibboleths that resonate with this memory: the narrator falls for a man who is visibly other and is subsequently

---

[3] By the time Suzanne's first known publications appeared in 1935, another Suzanne Dumesnil (Suzanne Dalbray, fl. 1902–26), a famous opera singer known for her dedication to Debussy, had long retired: confusion was no longer possible.

punished for it, thrown into the hell of a loveless, exploitative marriage and parental alienation. What we should acknowledge, ultimately, is that Suzanne's egalitarian convictions were formed in opposition to the beliefs prevalent in the French colonial society in which she grew up. She seems to have felt deep sympathy for decolonisation movements later in life; some shreds of information suggest that she carried a knowledge of how racism functions and expresses itself from her colonial childhood (JEK/A/7/47).

Paul's health remained poor and he died in 1921, aged forty, probably of tuberculosis, leaving a terrible void behind him. Suzanne was then studying at the Ecole Normale de Musique in Paris; she had left Tunis for Paris in 1918 or 1919. She and Andrée always kept happy memories of their father (AMC; MTW). Suzanne remembered especially fondly the long walks she would take with her father, hand in hand, in silence (JEK/A/7/27). Her memories echo Beckett's own memories of his father; perhaps Paul Déchevaux-Dumesnil, too, is present in *Compagnie/Company*.

After Paul's death, Jeanne found herself without resources. She found work in France, in Troyes, as governess and lady-in-waiting for a wealthy family, the Mauchauffées, for whom she worked until she became too elderly and too unwell. Her employers owned a large hosiery manufacture that also produced underwear and clothing. Their family home was next to the main factory in Troyes. It took Jeanne a long time to feel comfortable in this environment: after nearly twenty years of service, she confided to Andrée that she found life with a family who have never known hardship alienating. The wealthy, she observed, see the world completely differently (to Andrée, 8 June 1940). Andrée was in a more stable situation (Tholozan-Warluzel, 2024, 138). In Tunis, she had trained as a teacher and married a man from a Sicilian and Greek family, born in Tunis, with a good situation in banking. Teaching provided a lifeline when the marriage ended fifteen years later. She moved alone to Zarzis in the Tunisian south, learnt Arabic and taught in a small school. She returned to France in 1957, the year after Tunisia's independence was proclaimed, and settled in Nice, which enabled her to visit Suzanne in Paris more regularly. The two sisters shared a love of literature and the arts. Andrée, too, understood the significance and novelty of Beckett's writing from early on, as revealed in notes towards a critical commentary found in her papers by her granddaughter Michèle. Beckett, for his part, occasionally asked the Editions de Minuit to send books to Andrée and to a friend of hers in Tunis (Correspondance personnelle 1957–61, IMEC).

The letters and postcards preserved by the family show that solidarity reigned supreme (Tholozan-Warluzel, 2024, 150) and it was often thanks to one another that the three women got by. What also surfaces from their correspondence are enormous amounts of love, care and affection, manifest in the sweet names

Suzanne used for her sister until her early twenties and Jeanne's constant tenderness towards her daughters.

Suzanne, it seems, immediately loved Paris. The few photographs of her student years kept by Andrée and Jeanne reveal her rapid transformation into a fashionable Parisian with haircuts *à la garçonne* and well-cut, elegant outfits; she probably already knew how to sew for herself. Money was scarce, and she longed for little things from Tunis – including Minerva cigarettes, a Greek brand cheaper than Parisian cigarettes (Suzanne to Andrée, 19 September 1920). She frequented the museums and went to concert halls as often as she could, with friends such as Mita Tuby (JEK/C/1/149). A key event was Yehudi Menuhin's first concert in France in 1927, at the Salle Gaveau, which she attended with Andrée. The performance moved her deeply; Menuhin was then a child (Tholozan-Warluzel, 2024, 142). Other interests, in sculpture and painting, dominate her postcards to her sister in the early 1920s. Her messages are minimalist at best, but her keen interest in art history and irreverent humour come to the fore. Several postcards are photographs of marbles exhibited at the Petit Palais and the Musée du Luxembourg. The reproductions she chose – of Antonin Carlès's *Abel*, Léon Comerre's *La Pluie d'or* or François Sicard's *Agar* – convey her fascination for nineteenth-century reclining nudes in postures of total abandonment. On a postcard of Etienne Joannon's sculpture *Lassitude* (*Weariness*), she evokes a hotel where she appears to be doing cleaning in exchange for rent; she has lost so much weight that family friends have noticed it (to Andrée, 19 September 1920). An undated postcard, probably sent to congratulate Andrée on her engagement, features a reproduction of George Frederic Watts's *Love and Life*, an allegorical painting of love and life as struggling companions in hardship and starvation. Another undated postcard, probably sent for Andrée's wedding in 1920, features a reproduction of Jean Gautherin's *Le Paradis perdu*, with a protective Adam and a terrified Eve. Andrée – also fiercely independent – would certainly have laughed.

At the Ecole Normale de Musique, Suzanne was among the first students: the institution – a private school known today as the Ecole Cortot, unrelated to the Ecole Normale Supérieure – was created in October 1918 (Olivier, 2002, 11) and seems to have started running in 1919. An undated photograph shows her in a student cohort consisting predominantly of women (JEK/D/1/6/11). The premises were then a former private mansion at number 64, Rue Jouffroy d'Abbans. The founders, Alfred Cortot and Auguste Mangeot, persuaded influential professors from the Paris Conservatoire to teach there as a side hustle, which meant that the two institutions shared the same pool of expertise, although much teaching was done by delegate instructors (Taylor,

1988, 460). The aim was to rival German *Hochschulen* by offering an eclectic education according to French traditions (Charpentier, 1920, 1), while providing a better-rounded alternative to the system of relentless competition used at the Conservatoire (Taylor, 1988, 40, 561). The courses, oriented towards performance or pedagogy, covered all aspects of music and general knowledge pertinent to musicians and music teachers' careers, and assessment encompassed written examinations and live performances, allowing students to demonstrate depth of repertoire (40–1).

With its talks, recitals and progressive spirit, the Ecole Normale de Musique was an exciting place. In the professoriate, women were prominent; the first appointees included Marguerite Long, Blanche Selva, Wanda Landowska and Nadia Boulanger, later joined by Claire Croiza (Taylor, 1988, 460, 467). Suzanne became particularly fond of Isidor Philipp (Knowlson, 1996, 296), a legendary pedagogue whose methods centred on the quality of finger technique and focused on training versatile pianists (Timbrell, 1999, 79–90). At this stage in his career, Philipp had turned away from concert halls and dedicated himself to teaching, composing, music journalism and editing. Suzanne probably identified with his approach to music as an art involving the cultivation of personal skill. Her piano method, *Musique Jeux: Pédagogie moderne – Premiers contacts de l'enfant et de la musique*, defines music not as a social spectacle at which the performer must excel but as a pure source of personal fulfilment and a civilisational accomplishment. Music, she affirms in her preface, is 'the expression of our feelings' and opens heart and mind (Dumesnil, 1935a, npag). It is also 'a source of profound joy, of consolation, or fraternal union beyond all the limits invented by men' ('La musique est une source de joie profonde, de consolation, d'union fraternelle par-delà toutes les limites inventées par les hommes'; Dumesnil, 1935a, npag).

Students from all over Europe crossed paths at the Ecole Normale de Musique. By November 1920, over a hundred students from England, Switzerland, the Netherlands, Romania, Serbia, Scandinavia as well as Armenia and the American continent were studying alongside French students from the capital and the provinces (Charpentier, 1920, 1), which suggests that middle- and upper-middle-class families perceived it as a valuable alternative to institutions in Vienna, Berlin or Moscow. In student registers kept by Nadia Boulanger during the 1920s, Irish, British, German, Polish and Italian surnames are common (RES/VMC/MS-134 (1 2)). The teaching did not extend to modern languages, but the environment was so multicultural that it was probably informally multilingual. Suzanne does not seem to have learnt English there and probably learnt it later from Beckett; she knew enough to teach rudiments of English to a child in

Roussillon (Knowlson, 1996, 325). In her late fifties, perhaps later, she tried to learn English formally and took a Berlitz class, but allegedly didn't get far with it (Rosset, 2016, 123). Italian probably interested her more: during the 1970s, she kept an Italian dictionary within reach at home (AMC).

Suzanne's education shaped her musical tastes: all her life, she retained a deep love of the modern French composers who reigned supreme at the Ecole Normale de Musique. To her great-niece Michèle, she depicted her tastes as follows: 'Chopin, non, ce n'est pas mon truc du tout. Liszt à la rigueur et Schumann un peu. Bach bien sûr. Mais la musique que j'aime jouer, c'est la musique française Debussy, Ravel, et les autres ... Je déteste l'opéra vériste' ('Chopin, no, that's not my thing at all. Liszt if necessary, and Schumann, just a bit. Bach: of course. But the music I like playing is French music: Debussy, Ravel and the others ... I detest verismo') (Tholozan-Warluzel, 2024, 154). She always enjoyed live concerts and owned many records too (JEK/A/7/48). While her heart remained set on classical music, she was not dogmatic and appreciated good musical technique when she noticed it: for example, in later years she expressed the view that Michel Polnareff was a good musician (AMC).

Students at the Ecole Normale de Musique – as at the Bauhaus – were taught that artistic talent alone does not pay. Since only a privileged few would make a career as concert musicians, a key objective was to train music pedagogues capable of living from their teaching. Teaching is the route Suzanne took. She probably started at the Ecole Normale de Musique, since students there often taught too (JEK/A/7/24). Thereafter, she earned a living from private piano lessons to children and adolescents and gave more theoretical classes to music students – often informally, it seems. She gave harmony lessons to her friend Mita Tuby, for example (JEK/C/1/149). Another friend, Roger Deleutre (once a child prodigy on the piano), seems to have held a more formal post since he was identified as a 'young and eminent professor at our Ecole Normale de Musique' in *Le Figaro* in 1927 (De Crémone, 1927). Suzanne was never employed formally at the Paris Conservatoire either (her name does not feature on the staff registers);[4] the portrayals of her as 'a pianist at the Paris Conservatoire' (Brater, 1989, 38; Gordon, 1996, 133) cannot be accurate. The material and financial worries evoked in her letters to Andrée confirm that income was irregular and employment was precarious.

The information that survives about Suzanne's teaching dates from later, when she gave piano lessons for free to help out common friends, not from

---

[4] Thanks to Sophie Lévy at the Conservatoire National Supérieur de Musique et de Danse de Paris for confirming this.

when she taught assiduous pupils for a living. As a result, the anecdotes are conflicted and vague. The main source is Alexis Péron, whom Suzanne taught in 1940 or 1942, who had no interest in music and found her much too strict. He and his brother took revenge by exchanging unpleasant notes about her behind her back (JEK/A/7/67). With the Lindon children, in contrast, Suzanne had excellent relations; Irène Lindon, whom Suzanne taught later, was very fond of her (JEK/A/7/47). Her own piano playing became an intensely personal matter over time, although she and Beckett would practise four-hand pieces (Atik, 2001, 21). Her great-nieces never heard her play (AMC; MTW). Manolo Fandos is probably the only friend to whom she played the piano: 'I loved to listen to her', he recalls (Fandos, 2024). Playing alone in her friend Marthe Gautier's flat brought her great satisfaction. Alberto Chiarini once heard her because he eavesdropped at Gautier's door (he was impressed); otherwise, as soon as the bell rang, she stopped (JEK/A/7/19). In her self-effacement we may discern the influence of Philipp, who practised intensively alone but did not play for others outside of concert halls (he did not sit at the piano during lessons either, but sat next to his pupils) (Timbrell, 1999, 86). The time Suzanne spent in Roussillon without steady practice probably reinforced her need for privacy. During the 1920s, however, she certainly played with friends: Yvonne Deleutre, her friend Roger's sister, would sing to her accompaniment (Knowlson, 1996, 320–1).

Suzanne's letters and the few notes her mother made on the back of photographs contain shreds of information about where she lived. In 1920, as a student, she shared a hotel room (the cheapest accommodation in Paris was in hotels then) with a friend called Marcelle. In September 1925, she lived in a rented room on Rue de Pétrograd (now Rue de Saint-Pétersbourg) in the 8th *arrondissement*. In the late 1920s, she lived with her first companion, the pianist Georges Dandelot, in a flat he owned at number 7, Square de Port-Royal in the 13th *arrondissement* (BOB/28560, R/183615; JEK/C/1/149), close to her later residence with Beckett on Boulevard Saint-Jacques. Dandelot – also an accomplished athlete and competition runner – taught harmony at the Ecole Normale de Musique. Around that time, Suzanne adopted a small dog called Poucette, whom she cherished so much that her death in 1940 was a terrible blow (Tholozan-Warluzel, 2024, 148) (she was especially proud that Poucette was a mongrel; JEK/A/7/27). After the relationship with Dandelot ended, Suzanne lived in a flat in the 13th *arrondissement* (elsewhere, we can assume) that was large enough to entertain friends (Williams, 1989, 11). Her mother and sister kept a few photographs of places where she lived, including a photograph of a small ground floor flat with glass doors, a terrace and a dark interior, which cannot have been on Square de Port-Royal since those flats (in the Art Deco style) had been recently built and were bright, modern and spacious. Suzanne seems to have lived on Square de Port-Royal again later, since Beckett wrote a letter to Eugene and Maria Jolas from number 12 in February 1939 (Overbeck et al., 2024), and since a letter Suzanne wrote just after her move to Rue des Favorites tells Andrée to stop using her previous address on a square that remains unnamed (10 June 1940).[5] Moving would have been easy: Suzanne clearly owned the bare minimum. In 1933, she reminds Andrée of her promise of a blanket, to make her sofa less uncomfortable (29 October 1933). When the war begins, her first reflex is to go and get a sewing machine and a blanket from her mother in Troyes (18 September [1939]).

The relationship with Dandelot was important: Suzanne kept a large photo of him until the end of her life (JEK/C/1/149). For unclear reasons, which probably emanated from Suzanne, Beckett allowed Knowlson to relate how he and Suzanne had met in his biography (Knowlson, 1996, 94, 288) but made him promise not to name Dandelot (JEK/C/1/149). Dandelot, however, was the tennis partner with whom Suzanne played against Alfred Péron and Beckett at a private tennis club in 1929, when she and Beckett first met. She enjoyed playing tennis against men: with Edmond Tuby, Mita's husband, she frequented an indoor tennis court on Rue Saint-Jacques (JEK/C/1/149). She presumably liked swimming too, since there are photos of her on beaches and at the Piscine Molitor with Mita and Edmond (JEK/C/1/149; JEK/D/1/6).

What remains of Suzanne's relationship with Dandelot are two photographs, the odd family memory and brief mentions in interviews with Knowlson. Mita Tuby never went into Dandelot's flat but remembered meeting Suzanne on the street in Port-Royal, for evening walks with their dogs along Rue Saint-Jacques and towards Saint-Michel (JEK/C/1/149). Suzanne's mother knew about the relationship (MTW) and Dandelot was accepted by the family as her companion – enough to pose with Andrée's two children and Suzanne for a photograph probably taken by Andrée (Tholozan-Warluzel, 2024, 146). Here, Dandelot comes across as more affable and approachable than on official portraits of him as a composer and professor. On the other photograph, they look close, relaxed and happy, sitting by a beach in Houlgate with Suzanne's dog (146).

Dandelot was then separated – he had left his wife and young son in 1924, after four years of marriage (Dandelot, 2017, 12) – and the relationship with Suzanne probably started a few years before his second marriage. He is remembered as a brilliant pedagogue: his numerous solfège and harmony manuals, which appeared between 1927 and 1958 with prominent publishers such as

---

[5] Avigdor Arikha and Anne Atik later lived at number 9. It does not seem that Suzanne visited them there.

Henry Lemoine, Max Eschig and Alphonse Leduc, have been widely used ever since. His music has fallen into oblivion, but he saw himself as a composer first and foremost (AD). His compositions show a marked interest in literature (AD): he set a wide range of poems to music, from a twelfth-century *chanson de toile* to poetry by Apollinaire. While he undoubtedly had great talent, he also benefited from family connections, especially when his career began. His appointment at the Ecole Normale de Musique was a family affair: Auguste Mangeot, the co-founder, was his uncle (Dandelot taught there until 1942, when he became professor of harmony at the Paris Conservatoire). The premises on Rue Jouffroy d'Abbans also became the address of the thriving concerts business created by Georges Dandelot's father Arthur, and of *Le Monde Musical*, the magazine Arthur had founded with Edouard Mangeot (Auguste's father). Georges Dandelot undoubtedly had a strong rebellious streak: his separation from his first wife caused a scandal; he became a vocal pacifist; he set Pierre Louÿs's erotic *Chansons de Bilitis* to music (BNF MS-20035). But he belonged to a milieu in which one married within one's social class. In a family so eminent in the Parisian bourgeoisie, someone from a modest background like Suzanne, who was well educated but had no wealth and no family network, would not have stood a chance, no matter what artistic and intellectual affinities there were. The relationship broke down after a while, Mita and Edmond Tuby recalled with a chuckle (JEK/C/1/149). It seems unlikely that Dandelot's family were aware of Suzanne; in any case, the family archives for that period are non-existent (AD). Dandelot gravitated back to his milieu; his second wife, whom he married in December 1931, was Yolande Buisson, a poet and niece of the politician and Nobel laureate Ferdinand Buisson (Dandelot, 2017, 12). Their relationship had probably begun earlier, then stopped: a holograph score of Dandelot's *La Belle Yolande* dated March 1924 is dedicated to a real Yolande, the titular 'belle Yolande' (BNF MS-20007, 1).

It is in the mid-1930s, after the break-up, that Suzanne began to publish. Her piano method for children appeared in May 1935 with the prestigious Editions Henry Lemoine; on 30 June 1935, a short story by her, which I discuss in Section 4, appeared in the newspaper *Paris-Soir*. The short story, titled 'L'Amant de coeur', went unnoticed. The piano method did not: its novelty was praised in prominent music reviews such as *L'Art Musical* and *La Revue Musicale* (Gawann, 1936, 8; Martelli, 1936, 288). Evidently, the Editions Lemoine had deep faith in its value and were keen to invest in the design, typesetting and printing. The method comprises three booklets, focused on foundational theoretical, practical and pianistic notions, with blank sheet music, colouring pages and cardboard printouts. The cover – an unsigned black and white drawing of music notes with red lettering – is striking. The whole is dedicated to Arlette and Micheline Depret-Bixio, two sisters from a wealthy Parisian family, presumably piano students with whom Suzanne had honed her pedagogical practice. Although Suzanne mostly taught children of socially established families for whom piano playing was key to a child's education, her method affirmed that every child ought to have exposure to music. Her ambition was to support 'the average child' capable of 'loving, feeling, understanding music', regardless of any predispositions and without making assumptions (Dumesnil, 1935a, npag). Her colour-coding system, reminiscent of Maria Montessori's revolutionary methods (Tholozan-Warluzel, 2024, 143), allowed teaching to take place without an actual piano – which made the method usable in difficult circumstances in Roussillon (Knowlson, 1996, 325–6).

The form of *Musique Jeux* resembles that of Dandelot's manuals, which are commentary-led and rely on short paragraphs and frequent italicisation. Perhaps Dandelot facilitated contact with the Editions Lemoine, since he was one of their authors. But nothing suggests that Dandelot had input into the content of Suzanne's method. His manuals are renowned for being dry, and *Musique Jeux* is emphatically different. Suzanne's aim is to encourage autonomy through play and enable children to develop their own relation to music. Pure play, she affirms, does not suffice: one must appeal to children's intelligence and taste for difficulty. The theoretical definitions are limpid yet sophisticated; take, for example, her differentiation between pure noise ('souvent désagréable, presque toujours nécessaire'), musical noises ('agréables à entendre, mais impossibles à reproduire exactement sur un instrument de musique') and real musical sounds ('voix chantées, sons exécutés sur un instrument [...] qui peuvent être reproduits exactement sur d'autres instruments ou par d'autres voix') (Dumesnil, 1935a, npag). Silence is depicted as a necessity in music, as in speech and reading ('Les arrêts en musique, comme en langage, en lecture, en toute chose, sont nécessaires. Ils indiquent une respiration') (Dumesnil, 1935a, npag).

On the photographs of Suzanne as a young woman, her happiness and appetite for life are evident (Tholozan-Warluzel, 2024, 141–9). All the anecdotes point to a life filled with exciting encounters and friendships. The artists she got to know included the violinist Alexander 'Sasha' Schneider, of the Schneider String Quartet, who apparently had a crush on her: he remembered her as 'a beautiful blonde' (Atik, 2001, 48). She also befriended Heinrich Heidersberger (then a surrealist painter freshly out of Fernand Léger's Académie Moderne, who was becoming interested in photography) and a music student called Ida Karamian, long before she became the celebrated photographer Ida Kar (Williams, 1989, 11). Kar, who was Armenian but was born in Tambov, had lived in the USSR, Iran and Egypt before moving to Paris in 1928 to study medicine and chemistry; after six months, she turned to the violin and singing, until she lost her voice and realised that she would never be a great singer (Vines, 1962, 200). It is during this sensitive time that Kar befriended Suzanne and that her deep interest in socialism also began. In a flat where Suzanne lived in the 13th *arrondissement*, Kar met Heidersberger; this encounter triggered her discovery of photography and the start of her life as an artist (Williams, 1989, 12). Suzanne also befriended the Italian painter Adolfo Saporetti, one of the young painters of Montparnasse, who is mentioned affectionately in some wartime letters to Andrée. Like Kar, Saporetti was a free spirit who did not compromise. An early portrait by Nesto Jacometti presents him as a pure soul who managed alone, without courting attention or support, and spoke in striking ways about painting and composition (Jacometti, 1934, 199).

The facts that can be salvaged show that Suzanne gravitated towards people who were on the margins and could not take the future for granted. Her friends seem to have been mostly foreign (Roger and Yvonne Deleutre were exceptions) and included several Jewish exiles. For example, Mita Tuby, née Shulamit Khayenko, was from a Russian (probably Ukrainian) family and came from Tel-Aviv; Edmond Tuby, born in Alexandria, came from an Egyptian Jewish family. Suzanne also befriended Mita's brother, Izhar Khayenko, who later became an architect and was probably a student at the Urbanism Institute of the University of Paris in the early 1930s. In a confused interview shortly before her death, Mita speculated about a relationship between Suzanne and her brother (JEK/C/1/149); what is clear from Suzanne's surviving letters is that there was a lasting friendship and that Andrée knew Izhar too (Mita is not mentioned; Izhar was already a friend in 1933). Another friend whose identity is untraceable was called Génia (Suzanne to Andrée, 29 October 1933). Later friends, untraceable again, were called Tania, Lotti, Nandi.

Much of Suzanne's time before the war was spent in cafés. When she looked after her nephew Yvan, Andrée's son, when he was a child, she would take him around the Montparnasse cafés – which he loved (AMC). Thereafter, she continued to frequent the Left Bank cafés (Fandos, 2024); in her seventies, she still liked to drink *café-crèmes* (AMC). At the Dôme or the Select, in 1932 probably, Suzanne met someone with whom she formed a lasting friendship: Ruth Stern (later Ruth Salzman), a painter from the Saarland who was working for Léger in his Montparnasse atelier on Rue Notre-Dame-des-Champs (CS). The Montparnasse cafés were powerful melting-pots; the Dôme, Richard Whelan reminds us, functioned as 'émigré center, meeting place, employment bureau, forum for the latest ideas, and home away from home of the avant-garde' (Whelan, 1985, 54). Ruth, for her part, befriended an extended group of émigrés that included Gerda Taro and Endre Friedmann, better known as Robert Capa (CS). She had previously studied at Saarbrücken's art school with Fritz Grewenig and Oskar Trepte and at the Bauhaus with Paul Klee (CS; Scharwath, 1999, 203–4; Scharwath, 2017, 1027–8). Her studies unfortunately coincided with Klee's departure and the Bauhaus moving from Dessau to Berlin-Steglitz, where facilities and staff were under relentless pressure from the Nazis (Geelhaar, 1973, 15, 17; Wick, 2000, 48–9). Armed with a letter of recommendation from Klee, she settled in Paris and worked for Léger until the war began (CS). Ruth, a staunch feminist, thought the world of Suzanne: in her opinion, French women did not stand their ground enough and Suzanne was an exception (CS).

Suzanne's knowledge of contemporary painting can be linked back to this fruitful period. In her eighties, she could spend hours looking at an abstract painting and could explain the dynamics of abstract composition in clear, vivid terms (JEK/A/7/27). This understanding of painting was as much tied to a sharp visual instinct as to a whole education garnered at the contact of painters. Ruth Stern, for example, lived and breathed painting and taught much about visual composition to those around her (CS). She had such a good eye that she was able to spot a fake straight away; yet painting remained for her a secretive, personal activity and she would show her paintings only to her husband André Salzman during his lifetime (CS).

In 1935, Suzanne travelled with Ruth to Lebach, the Sterns' hometown, on the occasion of the referendum on the reattachment of the Saarland to Germany (CS). This is probably where she met Ruth's brother Paul, with whom a relationship developed (CS; Beckett, 2011, 44 n1). Paul Stern and his brother had been militating for the status quo (Stern, n.d.). In the wake of the referendum, owing to their anti-Nazi beliefs, the Sterns were stripped of their German citizenship and became stateless (CS). They joined Ruth in Paris, where Paul founded a small hat-manufacturing business (Stern, n.d.). He held a Nansen passport for an undetermined period of time and so did his mother Emma (CS; Stern, n.d). Suzanne had long been aware that nationalities can be withdrawn: in accordance with French legislation, her sister Andrée had lost her French citizenship upon her marriage to an Italian citizen in 1920, then regained it three years later when he was naturalised as French (Tholozan, n.d.), at the same time as large numbers of Spanish and Italian nationals settled in Tunisia. While the Sterns' situation was, of course, different, Suzanne was clearly sensitive to their plight. How long the relationship between Suzanne and Paul lasted is unknown; what is certain is that Suzanne cared deeply for the Sterns. After the war, Beckett and Suzanne spent several holidays at Ruth and André Salzman's house in Eure-et-Loir, notably in October and December 1946 (Overbeck et al., 2024). There, they both wrote. As a child, Claude Salzman would visit Rue des Favorites and feed the pigeons with Beckett; together, they would watch the employees of the Centrale des Chèques Postaux filing cheques next door (CS).

The details emerging from Suzanne's life during the 1930s point to a great deal of joy as well as hardship, and to a bohemian milieu where political sensibility was shaped by experience more than theory. Most of Suzanne's friends, it seems, found themselves in danger, often without papers, sometimes stripped of citizenship and other rights, or close to someone in a precarious situation, during the war especially but, sometimes, before that. This was a milieu on the left for sure, but unconventionally so in light of French parameters at the time. When Beckett referred to those friends of Suzanne's whom he got to know early on, he emphasised that many of them were Communists in ways suggesting difference, suggesting that his own friends were not that (Knowlson and Knowlson, 2006, 36). His casual remark doesn't convey the level of danger that card-carrying Communists would have faced in a context marked by forced exile and ostracism. Paul Stern is believed to have joined the Saar Communists while in Lebach (Stern, n.d). André Salzman, whom Ruth met in late 1940, and whom Beckett assisted with his early Resistance activities, was indeed a proud Communist, and was Russian and stateless (CS). Saporetti's father, Cesare 'Bomba' Saporetti, was a political exile fiercely opposed to Mussolini and a vocal socialist (David, 1973). Overall, there is no evidence that Suzanne 'had been in the Communist movement' as Cronin affirms (Cronin, [1996] 1997, 326). The details of her friendships and environment suggest more complex political ties, to an émigré Communism and a bohemian Communism that were not of the blue-collar kind for which towns like Argenteuil were renowned. Perhaps Cronin had heard the traditional phrase *compagnon de route*, used for long-standing sympathisers of the French Communist Party who were not necessarily card-carrying members; again there is no proof that Suzanne was ever that. However, that phrase has often been applied to Monique Haas, Suzanne's later friend. In short, those friendships with Communist sympathisers that had struck Beckett when he met Suzanne continued thereafter.

The residual information hinting at Suzanne's political views is not solid enough to allow for anything other than conjecture. What is certain is that she was always modern in her orientation – more so than Beckett, according to Jérôme Lindon and her great-nieces (JEK/A/7/47; AMC; MTW). She was firmly at home in the present moment but kept an eye on the future. Hermine Karagheuz, Blin's partner, had fond memories of the elderly Suzanne, who, she felt, had remained strikingly young in her ways of seeing and relating to the world (JEK/A/7/42). Lindon's and Chiarini's recollections suggest that she was leftward of Beckett politically (JEK/A/7/47; JEK/A/7/19). The facts certainly point to her keen sense of political responsibility and strong moral compass. It was she who kept Beckett and Alfred Péron in check when they discussed Resistance information without taking precautions (Knowlson and Knowlson, 2006, 81). It was she who asked Marthe Gautier to hide copies of Henri Alleg's censored book *La Question* in her kitchen during the Algerian War of Independence (MG). It was she, not Beckett, who would talk about decolonisation or about Palestine with Lindon when Lindon's political commitments determined the direction of travel at the Editions de Minuit (JEK/A/7/47). If the information from the 1930s is less conclusive, this is because the context was less fraught with danger and the sources are sparse. But there are signs that Suzanne's moral and political conscience was fully formed long before the war erupted. Her preface to *Musique Jeux*, for example, presents music as uniquely capable of developing kindness and sensitivity, not simply in children but in all human beings, by allowing them to become attuned to the world and to others. While the belief in the inherent good of humanity briefly expressed in *Musique Jeux* may have been short-lived, these are clearly the views of someone who wanted to overcome established ways of thinking – or what she called 'the limits invented by men' (Dumesnil, 1935a, npag). The picture that emerges, ultimately, is that of someone who stayed a few steps ahead and went about doing things in her own way.

What is known of the younger Suzanne points to her low interest in keeping up appearances and her even lower interest in abiding by the social expectations imposed upon women of her generation. By the time she became Beckett's companion, she had worked hard to allow her life to be driven by her own artistic interests and ambitions and had broken the mould of many common social expectations. She wrote, she published, she helped others – from her piano students to Ida Kar – understand their artistic potential. With her modest origins, she was probably the first genuinely self-reliant woman Beckett got to know (he otherwise frequented and fell for well-off and wealthy women). The Suzanne with whom he started a relationship in 1938 may have left few traces, but everything that is known discredits Peggy Guggenheim's rendition of her as a motherly curtain-maker with whom Beckett would soon vanish into 'a workmen's building' on Rue des Favorites (Guggenheim, 1980, 184). Life with me would not have been that, Guggenheim suggests (Beckett's address, she reports, 'made everyone [among her acquaintances] laugh') (184). Unfortunately, Guggenheim's account, with its evident contempt towards Suzanne's social class, has left enduring traces in biographical writing about Beckett, largely because it was formerly the only expansive source to evoke the early months of

Suzanne and Beckett's relationship. What is most surprising, in hindsight, is that Suzanne left behind so much of what she had built to look after Beckett's career and wellbeing after the war. What other lives would have been possible? How long could a woman without wealth hold back social expectations? How long could pure strength of character endure? There is much to speculate about, but the records are so fragmentary that Suzanne will no doubt keep her secrets.

## 3 Suzanne after Beckett, from 1938 to the War's Aftermath

The early months and years of Beckett and Suzanne's relationship have left the odd trace. Poems, which I discuss in Section 4, were written. There was a cat, whose death was devastating for Suzanne, and whom they buried near Rue Hallé (JEK/A/7/27). There was probably a shared friendship with the Polish painter Jankel Adler – an exiled Jewish artist belonging to the School of Paris – since Suzanne later kept a painting by him from 1938, next to paintings by Manolo Fandos, Henri Hayden and the Van Veldes, which clearly had sentimental value (Knowlson, 1996, 794 n150). There is one trace of life in the moment: pencil notes in Suzanne's hand on the back cover of a book belonging to Beckett – a copy of Descartes's selected works, *Choix de textes*, edited by L. Debricon. Suzanne's jottings, 'Danton 6268' and 'Lucien Lelong 3.15 / Av. Matignon / Depart. Edition' (Van Hulle, Nixon and Neyt, 2016), clearly date from before the war. 'Danton 6268' was a Parisian telephone number: that of the dancer and teacher Marie Kummer in 1929 and, in January 1938, that of Paul Leulliot, a *lycée* teacher and historian close to Marc Bloch and Lucien Febvre. Lelong was a celebrated French couturier. In his shop on Avenue Matignon, which also sold sewing patterns, a specific department was dedicated to 'Edition', an affordable fashion line launched on the principle that 'elegance is not necessarily a matter of money' and conceived to be tailored in one sitting (Campagne, 1937). The worlds colliding between the book's covers seem irreconcilable: the volume came from Jean Beaufret's library – and, as such, from the highbrow and virile world of the Ecole Normale Supérieure, where women were beyond rare and had no legitimate place. Beckett's world of reading is revealed as Suzanne's too, integrated into her world of doing. Suzanne's interest in philosophy has left other traces; think, for example, of her later gift of Geneviève Bianquis's *Nietzche devant ses contemporains* to Anne-Marie Colombard (AMC) and Pierre Chabert's recollection of her reading Maurice Blanchot two years before her death (JEK/A/7/33).

Shared artistic and intellectual interests were key to their relationship: their first activities involved going to concerts and exhibitions (Knowlson, 1996, 288). The circumstances are well known. They met again in January 1938, after

Beckett was stabbed on the street; his aggressor had a criminal record, as the Parisian newspapers covering the incident soon reported, and turned out to be a pimp. The stabbing, on 7 January 1938, coincided with Suzanne's thirty-eighth birthday. This is the point at which Suzanne makes a low-key, if not underwhelming entrance in biographies of Beckett (memorably, in Bair's biography, as 'a piano student'; Bair, 1978, 278), with the limelight remaining on the colourful and extravagant Guggenheim, with whom Beckett had been in an uncommitted relationship when he met Suzanne again. Beckett was then rather adrift and Suzanne visited him in hospital after reading about the stabbing. They became an item semi-officially that August, when they travelled to Normandy and Brittany to see Arland Ussher and Alfred Péron (Beckett, 2009, 578). Long after, in April 1939, Beckett informed Thomas MacGreevy of the existence of a 'French girl [...] [he] is fond of, dispassionately, and who is very good to [him]' (657). This oft-cited wording should be understood in the context of his interwar correspondence with MacGreevy, where the tone towards women could be disparaging. Suzanne, for her part, remembered Beckett as having been in an alarming psychological state at the start of their relationship (JEK/A/7/53). By April 1938, Beckett had moved to number 6, Rue des Favorites – Suzanne had probably found the flat for him (Guggenheim, 1980, 176). By early June 1940, Suzanne had settled there for good (Suzanne to Andrée, 10 June 1940). Rue des Favorites, formerly a passageway, was a new street created in the mid-1920s, but number 6 quickly amassed a history and character: miscellaneous facts and names show that the flats housed a diverse working-class population, the occasional Communist revolutionary (Georges Mercader, brother of Trotsky's assassin Ramón Mercader) and the odd painter (Dominique Manago before the war, Vu Cao Dam from 1942 to 1944) (Gallica, 2000–24; Maitron, 2007–24). Such an environment corresponds with the diversity that Suzanne seems to have craved.

If Beckett's letters seem guarded about Suzanne, hers are even more so. Initially, she informs Andrée that she is not alone in Paris because a friend has returned from Ireland and may be able to find civil employment owing to his Irish passport (18 September [1939]). Nine months later, when she gives her new address on Rue des Favorites, she explains that she is living with friends who are ready to leave Paris with her when necessary; she is already planning to go to Avignon, where Roger Deleutre's mother lives (10 June 1940). The following month, from Arcachon, she relates her momentous journey with an unnamed friend in detail (6 July 1940). Jeanne, she reports, is in Arcachon too with the Mauchauffées, her employers, but in the Abatilles neighbourhood, and she sees her nearly every day. Suzanne probably visited her mother alone: Jeanne does not seem to have met Beckett before her trip to Roussillon in the winter of 1943 (Knowlson, 1996, 331–2). Then, in letters from 1941, Beckett is named, but as someone for whom Andrée acts as relay by forwarding letters from Tunis, as she does for Saporetti (Suzanne's wordings show that Beckett's letters to his mother in Dublin transited through Andrée). Finally, in a letter from 5 October 1942 sent from Avignon, Suzanne acknowledges Beckett as her companion; in a sequel from 13 October, she announces that a move to Tunis is on the cards, that she and Beckett are willing to consider marriage if it helps them escape and that she is now living off Beckett's family allowance – in the midst of what sounds like amused laughter and nearly in the same breath.

Strangely, what little remains of the correspondence between Beckett and Suzanne dates from this time of terrible difficulties with communication. Two drafts of loving letters from Beckett, from the exceptionally cold winter of 1941–2, feature among doodles and jottings in the *Watt* notebooks. They are partially written in code, recalling the codes Suzanne used with her sister, and reflect their awareness that sharing information in writing was unwise. Beckett encourages her to stay strong while they are apart. He reports that he has everything he needs; that the coat donated by friends keeps him warm; that he is keeping busy with writing, music and private lessons; that he has turned to woodworking to defeat the cold, has made a small chair and may make an identical one for her (Notebook 2, HRHRC). The family papers do not shed light on Suzanne's whereabouts, beyond indicating occasional visits to Troyes to see Jeanne (MTW). If Suzanne went elsewhere by herself, then this is the only trace.

The running thread in Suzanne's wartime letters to her sister is the scarcity of resources, although she expresses worry with her usual reserve. When the war breaks out, piano lessons become insufficient and she hopes to find work somewhere as a volunteer in exchange for food (18 September [1939]). Jeanne, for her part, looks upon the war's evolution with horror and lucidity; a nuanced and articulate letter-writer, she sends striking missives to Andrée analysing the political situation, lamenting the loss of lives and the plight of refugees (undated [1940]; 1 June 1940; 8 June 1940). Jeanne would have preferred for Suzanne to stay with her and the Mauchauffées but is aware that Suzanne's temperament and independence make it impossible for her to live in such a privileged and stultified environment (Jeanne to Andrée, 8 June 1940).

With each change of circumstance, Suzanne loses more of her belongings. By the time she moves to Rue des Favorites, she has lost nearly everything and is aware that what little she still owns will disappear (10 June 1940). In Arcachon, all she has left are her sewing patterns – but no matter, she says. She is eating well, and with her seaside tan she looks quite unlike the refugees upon whom everyone lavishes pity (6 July [1940]). She probably got on well with Mary Reynolds, a woman of immense talent, courage and foresight. Later letters from

Paris detail a darker life and mention unpredictable shortages and Nazi executions (11 September [1941]). A parcel from Andrée containing halva brings Suzanne to the verge of tears and reminds her of everything long lost (1 September 1941). Roger Deleutre, in Paris too, isn't managing either: he has become very thin and also depends on food donated by Jeanne (3 March [1941]). In Roussillon, the hunger is worse than expected and so is the boredom. In their rented villa, 'Les Roches Rouges', all the basics are missing. There is only a malfunctioning stove and there is no food to cook, not even potatoes (13 October [1942]). Suzanne asks Andrée to send parcels of pasta and couscous (29 October [1942]). Some time is spent daydreaming about Tunis, although they have learnt, she says, not to make any plans. Much seems invested in this idea of a new life in a safe haven – too much, perhaps, to ever enable a return. When she and Beckett took their only holiday in Tunisia, in 1969, they only briefly travelled through Tunis and avoided places familiar to Suzanne from her youth. Anything else would have revived old pains, we can surmise, and that is something Suzanne was never into: she left pain and disappointment behind – and she encouraged Beckett to do that too, in relation to Ireland particularly (MS 5519/1/1, f. 42). Later holidays in the Maghreb were spent in Morocco; her longing for lost days remained just that.

Suzanne's letters to Andrée are dominated by considerable gaps: the correspondence did not always get through and some of it has clearly disappeared. Several letters highlight Suzanne's awareness that her words will be read by third, unsympathetic parties. She names very few people. Nothing in her account of being in Vichy identifies the Joyces, for example, who remain unnamed friends among others (6 July [1940]). Later, she occasionally uses code names and pre-agreed sentences in the style of the Resistance. When real names are mentioned, they are Germanic or Slavic and become associated with departures and disappearances. It is impossible to ascertain what really happened to Suzanne's friends beyond what she briefly relates in her letters, but this very lack of information and the tentative, coded nature of Suzanne's allusions reflect on which side of the fence these friends found themselves when exile, severe hardship and internment became common realities. Izhar, whom Suzanne has seen regularly until her departure for Vichy, suddenly goes missing (6 July [1940]); her worry is evident (he probably moved to Argentina, since he later lived in Buenos Aires; as for Mita, she moved to Egypt before the war and later lived in London). In a letter dated 18 September 1939, Suzanne mentions that her friend Tania is pregnant and in Wilno (now Vilnius), and she reports that Tania's ex-husband and Lotti's ex-husband have joined the French army to defend France. In another letter dated 3 March 1941, she mentions that Lotti's husband is still in Paris but can no longer work because he is Jewish; that Tania's ex-husband Nandi (a common diminutive of Nandor) is a prisoner in Germany; that Yvonne's Deleutre's husband, Marcel Lob, has lost his teaching job because he is Jewish. She reports that one of her pupils is leaving for the United States, presumably on one of the rare exit visas available. Her former teacher Isidor Philipp, of Jewish descent, settled in the United States that year too.

The Sterns are mentioned in two letters. In July 1940, from Arcachon, Suzanne expresses worry about Ruth's mother, alone in Paris without her children. Emma Stern had joined the Parisian crowds on the roads during the *exode*, then decided to walk back home: she felt that, as a German woman, she had no reason to flee from the Germans (CS). Another letter to Andrée from March 1941 reports that Ruth and her mother have returned to Paris but Ruth's brother is in Marseille; he is right to stay in the free zone, Suzanne observes (3 March [1941]). Under these words different tragedies are concealed. Ruth had been detained in the Gurs camp for a whole winter but had managed to escape and waited some months in the South of France before returning to Paris (CS). Before getting to Marseille, Paul Stern had been detained in successive French internment camps set up for foreigners in the Mayenne department and the Loire Valley (Stern, n.d.). Marseille marked a moment of freedom; the following month, in April 1941, he was detained in another camp in Issoudun (Stern, n.d.). Thereafter, he returned to Paris with false papers and a gallicised name, lived with his new partner and had a daughter (Stern, n.d.). In September 1943, he was arrested while searching for a disappeared friend. He was sent to the Fresnes prison, then the Drancy camp, then Auschwitz on the last large convoy of deportees from Drancy. He had just turned forty-one when he was murdered (CS). An undated photo taken from identity papers shows a handsome man with expressive pale eyes and a hint of sadness in his gaze underlined by a half-smile (Stern, n.d.). We might wonder how much Beckett knew of the circumstances of Paul's death: it is in the Salzmans' house in Abondant that he wrote 'L'Expulsé' in October 1946, quickly, in nine days (Beckett, 2011, 28) – a text that deals with dispossession and loss, a return to a home that is no longer one, and a hat that is the legacy of a dead father.

The war experiences of Suzanne's Jewish friends and her concern for their whereabouts and welfare give a different dimension to the explanations Beckett gave when he attributed his decision to join the Resistance to witnessing anti-Semitic persecutions. Gloria SMH dealt with military intelligence, not with false papers or hiding places, and Beckett's recollections of the persecutions against Jews in France, which were vague and confused (Morin, 2017, 152, 154), correspond to the moment Gloria SMH was dissolved, rather than the moment he joined. It may well be that the friends he remembered were Suzanne's friends, whom Suzanne knew were in terrible danger. That the French laws on the status of Jews affected Suzanne profoundly is evident from her letters to Andrée, although as always her concern is expressed with utmost reserve.

The details of how and when Suzanne took action are fuzzy because, like many resistants, she did not speak about the war – not even to her family, with whom she remained very vague (MTW; AMC). In a letter sent during the escape to Roussillon, she just tells her sister not to ask questions and promises an explanation in person one day (5 October [1942]). Later, however, her friend Ruth would talk to her son Claude about this period, particularly about how she had to live under false identities. After the war, she took the name Susanne – in recognition, she said, of what Suzanne had done for her during the war (CS) – and her name upon her death in 1995 was Susanne Ruth Stern (Insee, 2019–25). She would tell her son how Suzanne had made false papers for her and her mother thanks to official stamps she had access to, probably in 1940 (CS). Owing to this story, Claude Salzman always thought that Suzanne came from a family of civil servants (CS). The false paper kits distributed by the Resistance were not yet circulating then, and using authentic stamps and materials would have been extremely dangerous, no matter whether this was done in isolation or in collaboration.

It is too late to know the truth. What is known is that, through Suzanne's friendship with Ruth, Beckett befriended André Salzman and acted as courier for him in Paris. Salzman was then producing and disseminating underground publications on his own initiative, and Beckett was useful to him because his Irish passport allowed him to circulate at night without an *Ausweis*, the special permit otherwise needed after the curfew (later, in 1943, when Beckett and Suzanne were in Roussillon, Salzman undertook more dangerous actions for the FTP-MOI) (CS; Beckett, 2011, xvi).

There is no doubt that Suzanne was involved in Beckett's activities in Gloria SMH, although her contributions have been sparsely acknowledged. Beckett himself gave different accounts. In published interviews that touch upon Resistance action with Israel Shenker and with Knowlson, Suzanne is not mentioned. To Richard Stern, in 1977, he discounted Suzanne's contribution to Resistance work: 'The woman who's now my wife wasn't in it, but she came with me' (Stern, 1991, 185).[6] The contrast with his later interview with Lamont ('Suzanne and I worked in the Resistance'; 'Our group') is stark (Lamont, 1995, 34). A letter Beckett wrote to the French authorities in October 1945, while in Saint-Lô, certifies that Suzanne assisted him with his Resistance work and took the same risks as him, and identifies Jeanine Picabia

---

[6] It is always difficult to tell how much rewriting went into such interviews, which were cast on paper after the actual encounter, never during, and belonged to the realm of what Beckett called the 'friendly chat' (Hebert, 1980, 11).

as the authority capable of confirming. The letter speaks on Suzanne's behalf: Beckett affirms that Suzanne is not looking for recognition or special status, only for permission to look after his affairs in his absence. He concludes by stating his hope that she will be allowed to do so since she has already done him innumerable favours (JEK/A/3/77/13). The acknowledgement seems addressed to Suzanne, not the FFI officers to whom Beckett is writing. Suzanne's occultation becomes explainable if we look at the wider context: the contributions of the majority of French women to the Resistance were not officially recognised until fairly recently. Yet, as a large mass of oral histories and testimonies collected over the past twenty years indicates, the work always consisted of small actions, small solidarities in which whole networks including women and children came to life.

The war marks the moment when Suzanne is at her most loquacious as a letter-writer: the more life returns to normal, the more elliptic her messages to her sister become. The postcards sent after the return to Rue des Favorites merely indicate that Andrée is shipping Tunisian oranges whenever possible and that cleaning the flat was a major undertaking. Beckett's post-war correspondence is just as laconic on the subject of their life together: a few letters to Georges Duthuit mention that Suzanne has sent him a packet of Gauloises cigarettes inside a bundle of newspapers during a sad and difficult stay with his mother; that she has embarked on some ambitious redecorating during a stay in Ussy-sur-Marne; that she has painted their first wheelbarrow red (Beckett, 2011, 83–4, 192, 269). Beyond those anecdotes, her name crops up predictably in concluding greetings to a few close friends, and she is mentioned as his representative in letters about publishing contracts and theatre performances. That she became routinely overburdened over time is apparent from Beckett's reports on her varying levels of tiredness and exhaustion; gradually, to some friends, she is only portrayed as struggling, often unwell. From other evidence we can infer that Suzanne's temperament changed as the years went by, that some aspects of her character hardened and her need for privacy increased. But some constants remained: she keenly preserved her independence, she was appreciative of unusual personalities, she cultivated her friendships – and she continued to write.

## 4 The Writings of Suzanne Dumesnil

Everything to do with Suzanne's writing is fragmentary. Yet the miscellaneous dates of writing or publication that can be harvested from her texts – 1935, 1938, 1947, 1949, 1968 – suggest that she wrote throughout her adult life, as do the texts themselves. This impression is confirmed by the way in which, at the age of seventy-eight, she encouraged her great-niece Michèle to write and emphasised the benefits and fulfilment that writing brings (Tholozan-Warluzel, 2024, 156–7). From her perspective, hers was an issueless situation: with Knowlson, Jean Martin discussed – elliptically – Suzanne's deep awareness that writing would remain a hopeless dream (JEK/A/7/53). Edith Fournier probably got close to the root cause of that feeling: she observed that being perceived as someone who was trying to bask in her husband's glory was an unpalatable prospect for someone like Suzanne (JEK/A/7/27). She certainly refused to make concessions; Denise Deleutre saw this as key to her character (JEK/A/7/24). The purpose of this section is to summarise what currently survives of Suzanne's writings (readers should remember that copyright restrictions prevent direct citation) and discuss the peculiar itineraries of her texts wherever possible. What distinguishes Suzanne's texts is not simply their experimental persuasion but their close attention to everyday life, feelings and ways of speaking. The darkness – for plenty of darkness there is – is unlike the darkness for which Beckett's writing is renowned. The isolation and estrangement are socially determined, tied to the lowly status of women and children, condemned to be dominated yet finding some reprieve in the worlds of thought and the imagination. The narrators, in her post-war fiction, are always women; some pay a high price for refusing to comply with social expectations but also discover some form of freedom in adverse circumstances.

That Suzanne wrote was never a secret, although her family knew only of her piano method (MTW; AMC). Those who were aware of her literary work included close friends such as Martin and Gautier as well as the next circle of friends – Jacoba Van Velde, Bram Van Velde, Avigdor Arikha, Marcel Mihalovici, Duthuit and Lindon – and of course Beckett, who sometimes commented on her stylistic finds in his correspondence. Beckett would type up Suzanne's manuscripts because she disliked typewriters and typing, as Fournier later explained in fraught correspondence over the 'Petit Sot' poems (JEK/A/3/68/6). He often kept a carbon paper copy of her typescripts but sometimes lost the manuscripts, to Suzanne's dismay, leaving her with incomplete sets of documents (JEK/A/3/68/6). The French original of 'F–' was probably one of the texts by Suzanne that Beckett lost. Occasionally, he tucked copies of her typescripts into his books: on two separate instances, poems from her 'Petit Sot' series were found in unexpected places (see Atik, 2001, 7; Fernández, 2025, 29).

In the last years of her life, Suzanne threw away most of what was left of her writings and belongings; so much disappeared, Fournier noted, that what is there gains added significance (JEK/A/7/27). She gave some of her poetry and short fiction to Gautier and Fournier – clearly, in the hope that these texts would be further preserved – and, prior to that, to Bram Van Velde and Mihalovici (JEK/A/3/68/6). 'Quatorze poèmes' ('Fourteen Poems'), 'Françoise', 'L'Amarre' ('The Mooring'), 'A la Corbeille' ('In the Bin') and 'Contre-jour' ('Back Light') have survived those culls and were clearly close to Suzanne's heart; these typescripts, once in Fournier's possession, are now in the archives of the Beckett International Foundation in Reading (MS 5885/1–5). The *Transition* archives in Paris include a second copy of 'L'Amarre' and a short story titled 'Les Vieux Pas' ('The Old Steps'), in a folder containing texts Duthuit did not publish (DUTH 36). Of 'F–', the short story by Suzanne published in *Transition* in an English translation by Beckett, what remains are publicity notices naming Suzanne Dumesnil (DUTH 36), the typescript and proofs of Beckett's translation, and a typescript of her biographical note, all identical to the published versions (DUTH 40). Of another text probably written in or just before March 1949, all that survives is a sentence Beckett cites appreciatively to Duthuit, 'Ici est tombée face au temps la jeunesse de . . . . . Halte.' (Beckett, 2011, 121). We will never know precisely how much was discarded and lost. That other, as yet unknown typescripts are or once were in private hands is most likely, given Suzanne's propensity to give things away, and given how much her attachment to her writings seems to have fluctuated. She was stoical about her piano method having fallen into oblivion, although she continued to use it in her teaching. 'Ça n'a pas marché' ('It wasn't successful'), she said to Anne-Marie Colombard, with a flick of the hand suggesting that bygones should remain bygones, and that nothing could be done to mitigate the brutal interruption caused by the war (AMC). But total detachment is unlikely. When I met Gautier over a decade ago, I asked tentatively about Suzanne's writing, whether I was right to think that she wrote a lot more than is commonly assumed. Gautier did not answer directly (she was the most loyal of friends) but intimated that there had been a lot of writing indeed, together with a lot of frustration and sadness.

Much suggests that Suzanne saw writing as she saw music – as a source of personal fulfilment – and much also suggests a counter-tension: during the late 1930s and the 1940s, she clearly wrote with publication in mind. Her typescripts are presented as ready for publication in the visual conventions of the period. Her annotations – to 'A la Corbeille' in particular, which features the largest number of changes – show that she was a careful proofreader and a demanding editor, who checked rhythm above all things. Paratextual information is otherwise scant. Three typescripts bear explicit dates: 'Françoise', dated Abondant, 18 November 1947 (hence completed during a holiday without Beckett at the Salzmans' house); the version of 'L'Amarre' held in Reading, dated 25 January 1949; and an untitled poem dated 16 September 1968. 'Françoise' and 'Contre-jour' show that Jacoba Van Velde represented Suzanne for a time and was not just Beckett's agent: her name (as Tonny Clercx) and Paris address appear on the first page.

Suzanne's writings also show that she was a lucid reader, knowledgeable about contemporaneous writing trends and literary representations of women in the *longue durée*. About her reading tastes little information survives because of her reluctance to accrue belongings – a reflex probably inherited from the war, when anything could vanish without notice. She liked to give away the books she enjoyed, to Edward Beckett and Anne-Marie Colombard, for example (Gussow, 1996, 117; AMC). The books she gave to Anne-Marie included August Strindberg's play *La Danse de mort* (*The Dance of Death*); Emmanuel Bove's novel *La Coalition*; André Lang's biography *Une vie d'orages: Germaine de Staël*; James Joyce's *Dedalus* (the French translation of *A Portrait of the Artist as a Young Man*); and Geneviève Bianquis's *Nietzche devant ses contemporains* (AMC). She liked to discuss the writings of Cioran and Pinget, and Jean Genet's *Les Bonnes* (AMC). There is also in Beckett's library a 1922 edition of Dostoievsky's *La Confession de Stavroguine* in a French translation by Ely Halpérine-Kaminsky that bears Suzanne's name (Van Hulle, Nixon and Neyt, 2016). Louis-Ferdinand Céline was an important author for her; 'she loved his writing', Anne-Marie Colombard recalls, and she refused to believe that Céline was anything other than a profoundly good and generous man: this fact was for her proven by his practice of medicine and dedication to the poorest and most deprived (AMC). This view, then dominant, had been ardently cultivated by Céline himself since the start of his literary career: he presented himself as a doctor above all other things, as 'le médecin des pauvres', the doctor of the poor (Labreure, 2000, 37). Unsurprisingly, Suzanne loved Henri Michaux, a writer known for his experiments with brevity and with word and image; she found him very gifted and original (AMC).

Her own typescripts, too, reveal a fascination with the aesthetic of the fragment. The poems included in 'Quatorze poèmes' are between four and sixteen lines; 'A la Corbeille' (undated) is a page and a half; 'L'Amarre' a little over two pages; 'Les Vieux Pas' (undated) two and a half pages; 'Contre-jour' (undated) a little over twelve pages. 'Françoise' (fifty-eight pages) is the longest text by far. The shortest stories, like the poems, experiment with their grounding in the present moment, while 'Françoise' retells a woman's life between her first love and what seems to be her last loss. All texts focus firmly on the quotidian, with dispossession and loss remaining key themes. 'Contre-jour' – thematically close in some regards to Beckett's post-war tales of wandering and homelessness – is a good example of this. The narrator is packing a suitcase very tightly and tries to take as many of her possessions as possible – a coat, a hat, some papers, a quilt, a spirit stove, a drawing board (to sit on, sleep and write, she says) and a dictionary. The scene – set in August – evokes the *exode* of 1940; others, too, are leaving with quantities of things to cover all eventualities, including hats. But her departure has another cause: this is the story of a woman who can no longer pay her bills, rent or food and is being evicted by her landlord. The elliptic ending sees her ponder the next steps and the possibility of finding refuge in a train station. 'L'Amarre' and 'A la Corbeille' strike a different, more experimental note, owing to their focus on the mechanics of narration and plot. In 'L'Amarre', the narrator is rummaging through her papers. Someone is calling, but she begs for more time. She finds a letter that her father wrote before her birth, along with his last letter to her before his death, and commits to burning them. She also finds poetry she wrote when she was young, which she dismisses as trite and embarrassing, and a letter she wrote to a man she had been seeing secretly, along with his first gift to her. By the time she has finished sorting through her belongings, there is no one left to respond to her – and in this ominous silence she utters what seems her last sentence. In 'A la Corbeille', the narrator is looking for someone to speak to, struggling with an excess of thoughts and lamenting the inability of words to do what they should and the confusion in her head (like the narrator of 'Françoise' when she begins to tell her life story). The closing scene, in which the narrator's body is dragged up to a wall, evokes an execution. She asks for her eyes to be covered but her voice is too low to be heard. Then she agrees to stop speaking altogether. Likewise, 'Les Vieux Pas' is shaped by moving thoughts and perceptions, first dreamlike, then nightmarish. The setting is more rural; the text begins with a likeness between the narrator's reflection of herself in a public fountain and her memory of her grandmother's face. The world, she observes, is full of the sounds and traces of steps, forever returning. All one can do is stand up and keep on walking, and she attempts just that.

Lived experience provides the background to some of Suzanne's short stories, as we can surmise from 'F–' (Cohn, 1998), which relates a flight and a search for safety and seems indebted to dangerous situations experienced on the way to Arcachon or Roussillon, or to stories of crossing the demarcation line heard from others. Other anecdotes and phrases evoke more precise experiences and character traits. The narrator of 'L'Amarre', for example, sees the past as a burden (MS 5885/5, f. 1). The narrator of 'Contre-jour' lived in a type of flat that Suzanne probably got to know well before the war and has a fine sense of hearing (MS 5885/3, f. 5, f. 9) (Suzanne had perfect pitch; Knowlson, 1996, 296). An expression attributed to the narrator's mother in 'Françoise' (meaning 'this is a pigsty') corresponds to something Jeanne Déchevaux-Dumesnil was fond of saying (MS 588/5/2, f. 4; MTW).

'Françoise', the centrepiece in what remains of Suzanne's writings, is intensely plot-focused – unlike the other texts, which rely on suggestion and rapid shifts between circumstances and conditions of narration. Over the novella looms a specific legal framework: the French regime of tutelage and deprivation of rights imposed upon minor and married women by the Napoleonic Code until 1938. The narrator is spending New Year's Eve alone in Paris. She reminisces about her past and her running thoughts periodically disrupt her account. The man she is living with, Emile, is probably unfaithful to her, but she accepts it. An unforeseen encounter with her former husband brings other memories back to life: the ill-fated, unconsummated affair she had as a schoolgirl, far away, with an older man – a married painter with children who was enough of an outsider (including racially, it is suggested) for their trysts to cause deep trouble. Someone sees them together; he is forced to leave for the United States; her family make threats; she loses control of her life. She falls under the domination of her brother's best friend, to whom she becomes engaged, then married. The marriage that could have brought opulence and freedom leads her to lose all independence and access to money of her own. Her despair is such that she fantasises about being offered refuge on a boat while wandering along the Seine. The birth of her first daughter, Gisèle, marks the beginning of a long process of estrangement; heavily sedated on morphine, she remains bed-bound while her mother-in-law takes over the care of her child and the running of the household. The passage depicting her disempowerment is harrowing; it is rare to see childbirth and its unique level of pain depicted with such sympathy. When she becomes pregnant with her second child, Lucie, she hopes for a boy – far preferable, she observes, to being a girl. Her bond with Lucie weakens when the child is taken away from her bedroom. One day, she goes to the cinema and stays out some of the night. Her husband accuses her of having an affair and leaves with the rest of the family. The word divorce is never uttered, but clearly a divorce takes place. The focus returns to the present of narration: she is waiting for Emile. They have been making plans to settle together for good somewhere near the Mediterranean, buy a piano, adopt pets. She waits and waits, then discovers while reading a newspaper that he was killed in a car accident. The article announcing his death identifies him as a single man. The lorry driver involved in the accident, a father of four, was not injured.

Suzanne's talent and commitment to writing are key to the jigsaw puzzle around Beckett's success and explain much of what is otherwise attributed to feminine intuition – why she believed in his writing when nobody else did, why she stayed with him through thick and thin, why she knew which publishers to approach, why she understood Beckett's attitude to the business of writing so well. She spelt things out more clearly and fully than anyone else in a letter to Lindon from April 1951, which reads as her own gloss over discussions they were having. What prevented Beckett from adopting the behaviour expected of him, she affirmed, was 'la crainte de la contrepartie' (Beckett, 2011, 242), the knowledge that each scrap of attention paid to him would have to be repaid in kind, by entering into endless conversations with supporters and agreeing to interviews and photographs, all of which constituted transactions that never ought to be part of the work of writing.

Suzanne's journey as an author was more eventful and unusual than these facts suggest: when she was younger, she had tried to work in a different mode, one in which writing is a transaction. Her short story from 1935, 'L'Amant de coeur', inhabits a resolutely middlebrow world: that of the 'Contes de *Paris-Soir*', in which writers are infinitely replaceable and are there to entertain. In 1935, *Paris-Soir* (a prominent right-wing newspaper) was one of the largest-circulation newspapers in France and its daily 'Contes' were especially popular (*L'Intransigeant*, its rival, launched 'Les Contes de l'Intran' in response). The *Paris-Soir* roster included budding writers who contributed a single story; established authors, forgotten today, who contributed more regularly (such as Eugène Dabit, Robert Dieudonné, René Pujol or Léon Lafage); and occasional women (such as Suzanne Martinon, Germaine Ramos or Léo Dartey/Henriette Stumm). The themes were provocative, so much so that the reactionary *La Revue des lectures* described the 'Contes' as pornographic publications that no respectable Catholic should read (De Lardélec, 1934, 270–1). Adultery was a key topic and this is what 'L'Amant de coeur' responds to. Suzanne's story is also a reflection on literary clichés about women and love, which returns to nineteenth-century French literature about Parisian women trying to forge their way through life. As detailed in novels about high-class prostitution such as Emile Zola's *Nana* and in Alexandre Dumas fils's play *La Dame aux camélias* (adapted from his renowned novel), the *amant de coeur* is the lover who does not pay. Elsewhere, the *amant de coeur* can be a penniless hopeful, an admirer who lives off the earnings of a courtesan under the guise of noble love, or a *souteneur* who lives off the earnings of a prostitute under less pretence. The plot in Suzanne's story recalls a passage from a study of prostitution in Paris by Alexandre Dumas père, *Filles, lorettes et courtisanes*: 'Thus every *amant de coeur* keeps watch over his mistress, not to ensure that she stays faithful, but the opposite: so that she does not attempt to fool him over the result of her disappearances: he follows her from the other side of the boulevard, or spies on her from behind a bollard' (Dumas père, 1843, 63).

At the heart of 'L'Amant de coeur' is a fascination for Parisian cafés. As in the rest of Suzanne's fiction, the narration is in the first person. While her later narrators are women, here the narrator is a man who enjoys observing women. The key themes – anything can happen in a café, coupledom is treacherous – are underscored by an illustration: a sketch of a generic Parisian café by Feder, who frequently illustrated 'Les Contes de *Paris-Soir*' and occasionally 'Les Contes de l'Intran'. We hear about the narrator's aversion to coupledom from the start: 'Un homme seul n'est jamais ridicule, pensais-je, il est lui-même. Tandis qu'à deux, il n'est plus qu'une moitié provisoire ...' ('A man alone is never ridiculous, I thought, he is himself. But in a couple he becomes no more than someone else's provisional half ...') (Dumesnil, 1935b, 2). A couple walks in. The woman – beautiful, elegant, lively – catches his attention. Her companion, assumed to be her husband, seems in turmoil and in mourning. The narrator follows them to a bus stop. The woman invites him to join her for a drink, then to a hotel room. But the hotel room looks cheap, and the narrator, uneasy, decides to leave. She begs him to stay and unravels her story: her home is across the road; she is a widow living on a large inheritance; the man from the café is her lover, and to make him happy she needs to keep him under the illusion that he is her *amant de coeur*. She has never had an affair, however, and all she does is wait a while. The narrator acts according to her wishes. He waits, then leaves, cursing fate, but concedes that he had to honour his word, play the role assigned to him until the end. The signature, Suzanne Dumesnil, introduces playful questions (who is this woman who speaks so confidently about men?) and reminds the reader that the mysterious woman is in control, not the narrator. The text shows the same taste for ellipsis, abrupt endings and external descriptions of sequential events we see in Suzanne's later short stories, and the narrative voice has the same poise and acidity. The sentences are not as rhythmical as in her post-war fiction, and there is more dialogue here than in her later texts, but we find the same alternation between simplicity and sophistication in the syntax; the same bravery with the idiosyncrasies of French tenses and grammar; the same unpredictable complexity in registers of speech – all of which, of course, are also hallmarks of Beckett's post-war writing style in French.

What otherwise survives of Suzanne's early writings is poetry: poems from the 'Petit Sot' series, including 'Les Joues rouges', and a previously unknown collection titled 'Quatorze poèmes', consisting of fourteen numbered and untitled poems. A separate typed copy of a poem from 'Quatorze poèmes' is dated 1938, which makes the set likely to date from 1938–9, at least in part (MS 5885/1). 'Quatorze poèmes' gives a good sense of Suzanne's range and accomplishment as a poet, not least because this cycle remains untainted by the misattributions that have plagued the 'Petit Sot' poems. These are poems about daily life which mirror the Parisian life evoked in Beckett's pre-war poems in French, but the technique and concerns are different. The form is distinctive: the poems attempt to work away from the sentence, to do without sentences altogether by eliminating punctuation. The technique is painterly, with each line adding a new layer of impression – the wind blowing, the aroma of a cup of tea, the smoke of a cigarette, the letters of Robert Schumann, a line from Jean de la Fontaine's fable 'The Grasshopper and the Ant'. There is less affectation, greater brevity and economy of expression than in Beckett's 'Poèmes 37–39'. Like the 'Petit Sot' poems, 'Quatorze poèmes' seeks to reach certain existential truths through an intense focus on the moment. The two cycles also share a focus on impending death and war and a lucidity towards the rhetoric of patriotism, manifest in allusions to men being sent to die on the battlefield and children being taught that warfare is a fact of life.

'Les Joues rouges' is the only holograph manuscript by Suzanne currently known; the other unpublished texts are typescripts. Authorship has been attributed to Beckett, although the facsimile published in Anne Atik's *How It Was* is evidently in Suzanne's hand. On the surface, there can be likenesses because Beckett's handwriting when he tried hard to make it legible can look a little like Suzanne's. However, having been brought up in different countries, they had also been schooled in different modes of cursive writing. Suzanne did not form many of her letters (b, d, g, j, o, p and t, notably) in the same way as Beckett. Her writing was not inclined to the right in the same way as his. Her hand had a different suppleness and would also tilt slightly when joining up certain letters in ways that Beckett's hand did not.

The misattribution was kick-started by Beckett: in 1960, when Arikha found the manuscript, tucked in a volume of Kant's *Werke* that Beckett had given to him, Beckett said that this was his first poem in French and that he didn't like it much (Atik, 2001, 7). He signed it without checking what it was, Fournier explains (JEK/A/3/68/6). Lindon and Fournier, both familiar with Suzanne's handwriting, formally identified the manuscript and other 'Petit Sot' poems as Suzanne's in correspondence behind the scenes, but Fournier was unable or unwilling to challenge Arikha and others more publicly after Lindon's death (JEK/A/3/68/6). Arikha, oddly, was well aware that Suzanne wrote and thought her a good writer, as did Atik (JEK/1/7/4); both were familiar with Beckett's handwriting but remained persuaded that 'Les Joues rouges' is in Beckett's hand. Beckett scholars have widely identified Beckett as the author of 'Les Joues rouges' too and his wayward signature has encouraged the perception that the other 'Petit Sot' poems in the archives are by him, despite how much their style and concerns differ from his. Interestingly, Ruby Cohn, who has otherwise dismissed the possibility that Suzanne could have been the author of anything, presents 'Les Joues rouges' as a stylistic 'tour de force' built on an intimate knowledge of the villanelle (Cohn, 2001, 99–100).

Clearly, what underlies the 'Petit Sot' poems is a broader writing process, to which Beckett briefly alluded in letters to George Reavey and Thomas MacGreevy between July 1938 and June 1939 (Pilling, 2015), at a time when he was unwilling to acknowledge Suzanne's presence in his life and keen to share his poetry with others. But Beckett's references to 'his' 'Petit Sot' in his letters are not necessarily evidence that the surviving typescripts are by him. Putting all the information back to back shows how some archived typescripts have been externally labelled as Beckett's without proof or indication of the rationale, generating, in turn, great confusion around poems that were originally Suzanne's, and unambiguously so. The resemblances with aspects of form, style and register in 'Quatorze poèmes' are evident. The 'Petit Sot', Fournier explained, was a character created by Suzanne, who haunted her for a long time, and around whom she wrote several variations situated at different stages of life (JEK/A/3/68/6).

The archived documents feature three interrelated cycles, tied together by a relationship recalling the pianistic genre of variations preceded by a theme. There are twenty-one poems titled 'Poèmes à Sam' ('Poems to Sam') in Bram Van Velde's papers, from the Jacques Putman archives. This set features two attributions to Beckett in Van Velde's hand, with one question mark (see Van Hulle and Verhulst, 2017). However, Van Velde cannot be seen as an authority on matters of authorship and style in French: his correspondence shows how much he struggled with the written word and how approximative his grasp of French grammar remained (Van Velde, 2012). Van Velde owned a copy of these poems because Suzanne had given it to him (JEK/A/3/68/6). At an undetermined point, Suzanne also sent typed copies of a series of poems titled 'Le Sot' to Mihalovici, in the hope that he would set them to music (JEK/A/3/68/6). Later, in 1985, Mihalovici gave these poems to Fournier, explaining that he had done nothing with them. Much suggests that this specific document has disappeared. Much suggests, also, that only a portion of the texts by Suzanne that Fournier got (from Mihalovici, then Suzanne herself, then Gautier) is currently archived (JEK/A/3/68/6). Clearly, many of the texts still in existence before Suzanne's death have disappeared since. How much will eventually resurface is anyone's guess.

In the archives, there is also a fax transmitted by the Editions de Minuit in 2002 with two different versions of twelve 'Petit Sot' poems (JEK/A/3/68/2); this document is not an original but a contemporary typed copy of the poems on two parallel columns. One batch (on the right) predates the other (on the left): that much is evident from poems on the left focusing on the Petit Sot hiding in a rat-infested attic or hoping to find a friend, which feature experimental variations on the themes and images set in their more literal counterparts on the right. The poems on the right are in the first person and bear individual titles; many are identical to poems in the Van Velde set. An unknown hand (Irène Lindon's, possibly) tentatively attributes this group of poems to Beckett, with inverted commas suggesting that the attribution is someone else's decision, or that the poems are generally said to be by Beckett. As with the Van Velde set, the attribution to Beckett does not come with information about the thought process followed or the evidence used, and contravenes the contextualising information provided by Fournier to which Irène Lindon nonetheless refers. The poems on the left are in free form and in the third person, and are described as belonging to a collection titled 'Le Sot' by Suzanne Beckett (however, because Suzanne did not call herself Suzanne Beckett as an author, this description partially comes from a third party). This more experimental series could be, or be related to, the set Suzanne sent to Mihalovici, since some poems look as though only minimal adaptation would be needed for them to be sung.

*Petit sot* – like *petite sotte* – is a consecrated term common in the nineteenth-century French Suzanne was fond of. It does not have the gentleness of 'little fool' or 'silly boy'; it is a verdict of stupidity without appeal (*espèce de sot* and *triple sot* are insults accusing someone of worthlessness). The poems are about the intense revelations that young children are capable of having. The central preoccupations might be summarised as follows: the 'Petit Sot' understands that growing up and behaving as he is expected to are the only solutions to the hardship of childhood, since getting older means escaping the label of 'sot'. But he also senses that the rewards promised for good behaviour are hollow and not worth the trouble. He immerses himself in play and in an imaginative world partially untainted by these realisations. In doing so, he discovers a spectrum of emotions – hatred, bravery, loneliness, sadness, frustration, fear – and becomes acquainted with the transitoriness of life and the ineluctability of death, be it natural or inflicted by war. This child is never naïve but is animated by a cold, lucid resolve, and each poem brings new insights into the development of his subjectivity and imagination. With the exception of 'Les Joues rouges', which is longer, brevity rules: some lines consist of a single word, some stanzas of a single line. The version of childhood offered here can be brutal (the Petit Sot makes all discoveries by himself), and in this sense the poems are full of sympathy for this little boy who battles universal problems alone. Evidently, these are not concerns we see in Beckett's writing from this period. The style, which has been depicted as overly simple and as coming straight from a child's mouth in critical readings attributing authorship to Beckett, isn't quite that: if we take a closer look, we can see that this child can be very articulate indeed, in command of multiple registers of language at once, and sometimes speaks from the vantage point of adulthood.

Many of the exercises Suzanne formulated in *Musique Jeux* involved variations around a theme or games of question and answer. Seen from this perspective, we can envisage a literary *quatre mains* around the 'Petit Sot' poems, a counterpart to the piano four hands Suzanne and Beckett liked to play together – with Beckett's part gone missing, and the initial impulse provided by a cycle of poems Suzanne gave him to respond to in verse. Given Suzanne's interest in pedagogy, given that, when their relationship started, Beckett's French was not as fluent as it later became, given how quickly he mastered extended registers of French after that, this seems eminently possible. Dirk Van Hulle and Pim Verhulst's recent discovery of modified lines from 'Le Petit Sot' (the first poem in the set Suzanne gave to Van Velde) in Beckett's hand, inside the back cover of a copybook of *Malone meurt* used between late 1947 and mid-1948 (Van Hulle and Verhulst, 2017, 211–13, 215), does not contravene this interpretation, and adds to the list of 'Petit Sot' variants found in Beckett's belongings (see Atik, 2001, 7; Fernández, 2025, 29). Suzanne returned to the 'Petit Sot' at various points; she was a talented poet and her poetry sticks in the mind; she and Beckett exchanged their texts (he typed hers; she corrected his); they discussed writing and assisted each other with publication.

Why Suzanne's handwriting on the manuscript of 'Les Joues rouges', so perceptibly different from Beckett's, has been seen as his seems strange indeed, but we can easily find explanations for this once we factor in the dominant representation of Suzanne in Beckett scholarship as someone who did not have what it took to write. Here, I simply want to highlight that this episode is revealing of the feeling of ownership Beckett could develop when the people close to him expressed artistic ambitions in realms in which he had expertise. Various sources indicate that he could be sharply interventionist. His collaboration with Pierre Chabert on a production of Pinget's *L'Hypothèse* involved radical cuts and transformations to the text (Chabert, 2005). When, at an undetermined moment, Jean Martin decided to write a novel (he was not inexperienced with writing: he had written screenplays including *La Bataille de l'eau lourde/Kampen om Tungtvannet* (1948) and *La Vie à deux* (1958), based on Sacha Guitry's original screenplay), Beckett allegedly bought him a large copybook, told him to write on the right-hand side and give the copybook back to him every day, to enable him to model on the left-hand side how writing should be done (JEK/A/7/53; this is not what happened to the Minuit document described earlier, however: the columns were created by a third party). The few mentions of Suzanne's short stories featuring in Beckett's correspondence with Duthuit – which speaks in the first-person plural and adjudicates between right and wrong – hint at a level of involvement that seems out of step with the context. 'Nous sommes très contents qu'<u>Amarre</u> vous ait plu' ('We are very pleased that you liked <u>Amarre</u>'), he writes in March 1949; however, this is not the title that should have been chosen, he says: 'Ce n'est pas ce titre qu'il faudrait' (Beckett, 2011, 117). Relaying one of Suzanne's good finds, he presents it as a 'jolie phrase', a pretty sentence (Beckett, 2011, 121). In later correspondence with Arikha about a 'little text' by Suzanne that he also really likes but that 'no one has ever noticed', the phrasing is double-edged too: 'Moi aussi, j'aime vraiment ce petit texte de Suzanne. Elle n'arrive que ce soir, elle sera contente que cela vous ait plu, personne ne l'a jamais remarqué' (Beckett, 2014, 54; the Editors of the *Letters* assume that this is Beckett's translation of 'F–').

That Beckett encouraged Suzanne to publish is clear: his translation of 'F–' in the January 1949 issue of *Transition* makes this evident. Although we can discern Suzanne's style if we peel away the Beckettianisms of the English version, the fact remains that Beckett's hand as a translator is all over that text, just as it is all over his translations from the early 1930s, late 1940s and early 1950s: he often took great liberties, his translation practice involved varying amounts of rewriting and he sometimes struggled to draw the line between translation and transformation (Beckett to Duthuit, 17 May [1949], DUTH 6). Suzanne, who cultivated detachment generally speaking, probably encouraged him to produce the best translation he could.

More importantly, a letter from Beckett to Duthuit indicates that a separate plan to publish a *plaquette* of Suzanne's texts was underway in the spring of 1949 (17 May [1949], DUTH 6). A *plaquette* is like a pamphlet: a short edition of collected texts, often poems, sometimes featuring drawings, generally stapled together without a glued binding. Michaux was fond of this format, as were smaller Parisian publishers such as Guy Lévis Mano for his Editions GLM after the war. Writing to Duthuit, Beckett asks for news about the progress of this *plaquette* with the *NRF*, the *Nouvelle Revue Française*. This is an interesting lapsus: although the *NRF* had published *plaquettes* before the war, the magazine was banned for collaborationism in 1944 and no longer existed in 1949. Gallimard published a monthly *Bulletin de la NRF* then, but it was an advertising booklet with notices, reports, the odd essay and occasional excerpts of forthcoming or reissued Gallimard novels. A Gallimard *plaquette* seems more likely: this format was occasionally used at Gallimard (Vignes, Huret and Les Libraires Associés, 2011). In the same letter, Beckett emphasises how deeply significant it would be for Suzanne to see her work published.

The three letters to Duthuit promoting Suzanne's writing, in their own peculiar way, should be thought of as exceptions. Of course, only small portions of life are recorded in letters, and the Beckett archives are very scattered. But in the correspondence I have encountered over the past twenty years, when

Beckett uses his contacts and reputation to support other writers, his attention is directed towards men and their prospects. I am not suggesting that he couldn't work with women: there were mutually rewarding exchanges with Barbara Bray and Edith Fournier in relation to translation (and, to a lesser extent, with Jacoba Van Velde),[7] and he nurtured important collaborations with Billie Whitelaw and Jocelyn Herbert around his plays. He encouraged Anne Atik to continue writing poetry at specific moments (Atik, 2001, 90) and supported Djuna Barnes when she found herself destitute (Nugent, 2023b). There is also ample evidence of a looser network of influence that did not involve direct contact (Nugent, 2023a). Nevertheless, delineating Beckett's perspective on women who published their own literary texts remains an awkward enterprise. From early on, he surrounded himself with women who wrote: we can think of Ethna MacCarthy, renowned for her poetry today; Mary Manning, who became a successful playwright early on; Nancy Cunard, whose achievements are well documented. Later, he corresponded assiduously with Mary Hutchinson and Kay Boyle. But it is difficult to guess from his letters that these women were writers. His correspondence does not come across as enabling for them, once we look beyond his tender, sometimes mildly flirtatious tone: he expected them to listen to and support him (similarly, with Bray, 'the help tilted in [his] favour', Sardin notes; Sardin, 2024b, 8). In his Parisian milieu, he knew very few women writers personally and traces of acquaintance are scant. Geneviève Serreau, Maria Le Hardouin and Diane Root feature in a select list he drew for the Editions de Minuit (February 1, 1957, IMEC), probably a guest list for the French premiere of *Fin de partie* at the Studio des Champs-Élysées. There is no evidence of his acquaintance with Le Hardouin elsewhere. He certainly corresponded with Root, a French-American writer and painter (Overbeck et al., 2024), and he knew Geneviève Serreau well and liked her personality. While he was fond of some of Marguerite Duras's texts, with Simone de Beauvoir and Nathalie Sarraute there was mutual and profound dislike. He also took exception to Jacqueline Piatier, an influential and assertive literary journalist (Cioran, 1997, 368). What Sarraute reported about Beckett during the war is troubling: 'Beckett couldn't bear that I had the least literary pretention. Even though at the time he admired enormously Simone de Beauvoir, my own aspirations seemed to annoy him' (Knowlson and Knowlson, 2006, 83). The dynamics with Suzanne were undoubtedly different, but this wider context cannot be ignored.

In theory, *Transition* could have been a passport for something else: the review was a well-oiled machine and Duthuit worked hard on its reputation.

---

[7] Beckett seems to have acted as intermediary between Fournier and Aidan Higgins to enable Fournier to translate Higgins, for example.

Review copies were sent far and wide, to whoever was thought capable of wielding influence, particularly in the US, and a system of reciprocal advertising was negotiated with American magazines including the *Sewanee Review*, the *Antioch Review*, *New Directions*, *Commentary*, *Story* and *Furioso* (DUTH 38) (in practice, publicity notices for *Transition* appeared in a wider range of publications). On a surviving notice in the *Kenyon Review*, Suzanne Dumesnil is named as a key figure in new French writing alongside André Gide, Pierre-Jean Jouve, Pablo Picasso, Jean Genet, Paul Eluard, Henri Michaux, René Char, Georges Duthuit and Jacques Prévert (Front Matter, 1949). Her name stands out: indeed, she is the only woman to have published fiction in Duthuit's *Transition*. Two other women appeared in the post-war *Transition* as authors, but not of fiction – the American poet Helen Burlin, author of a brief note on translations of Edgar Degas's sonnets by Richard Wilbur, and Gabriële Picabia, author of a text translated by Beckett recalling her memories of Guillaume Apollinaire. Clearly, some women submitted work to *Transition*, but it remains unclear who did so and what type of work was submitted. Duthuit's papers include typescripts by the American painter Charlene Goldenberg Palmer and the American poets Evangeline Zehmer and Carol Ely Harper (DUTH 38) – all in English, which precluded publication since *Transition* specialised in publishing English translations of French texts. The archives also show that Marguerite Matisse-Duthuit did large amounts of managerial and secretarial work unacknowledged, and probably editorial work too (the capital that propped up the review was hers). The records are piecemeal (Duthuit does not come across as someone who issued clear rejections; he probably preferred to stay silent and wait), but this is not a domain in which a woman writing under a woman's name was likely to flourish. Perhaps there were other soft rejections: Lindon, for example, seemed surprisingly knowledgeable about what Suzanne's poems looked like (Wheatley, 2002, 11). That no other publications followed in *Transition* must have been a blow, not least because the people running the review were familiar. Relations with Duthuit and his wife Marguerite were cordial and close. Max-Pol Fouchet, with whom Suzanne tried to have a dialogue over Beckett's work in late 1949, was one of *Transition*'s advisory editors, along with Jean Wahl, Eugene Jolas and Stuart Gilbert, whom Beckett knew directly.

It is unclear when Suzanne started to think that being 'Forgotten in musical, unknown in literary circles' (as the biographical note accompanying 'F–' presents her) was preferable to attempting to court attention (Duthuit, 1949, 151). Perhaps Suzanne worried about the transactions, constraints and compromises that any further attempts to publish with Beckett's friends would bring (Anne-Marie Colombard remembers her as someone who hated constraints;

AMC). Perhaps she became too busy: the correspondence held at the IMEC (mostly published) shows that much of her time and energy from October 1949 onwards was taken up with canvassing publishers on Beckett's behalf. Perhaps she felt too vulnerable to continue: in letters to Duthuit from 1948, Beckett portrayed her as struggling to come to terms with life continuing as normal in ways that suggested an existential, ethical crisis ('ne sachant ou donner de l'âme, lasse du silence, vite dégoûtée des mots'; 'inconsolable, au fond, de vivre'; Beckett, 2011, 83, 96). It may well be that Beckett's involvement – by translating 'F–', by orchestrating a possible *plaquette*, by commenting on her writing in conversations with others – was too much for her to bear. It may also be that seeing 'L'Amarre' and 'Les Vieux Pas' fall flat encouraged her to keep her writing to herself. In any case, Duthuit continually sought new authors and, although he repeatedly commissioned the same translators, he did not publish multiple pieces by the same authors.

The experimental bent of Suzanne's post-war fiction will invite analogies with Beckett's writing in times to come. There are Beckettian moments in 'Françoise' and 'A la Corbeille', with narrators unable to control their thoughts, complaining about words flowing out unstoppably or dying the moment they are uttered. But Suzanne's narrators are always women, which gives a different dimension to these moments, and her work has markedly different concerns. There is no doubt that there will be ongoing debates about their borrowings from each other; for my part I hope that these discussions will pay heed to Suzanne's role in shaping Beckett's literary language and approach to form. Suzanne's experiments with radically short fiction during the late 1940s correspond to a time when Beckett was not yet working in that form: 'F–', John Montague has observed, 'sounds like [Beckett's] later self' (Montague, 2001, 125). This could also be said of what survives of her poetry. A deeply striking poem by her, untitled and dated 16 September 1968, anticipates 'Comment dire', Beckett's last poem, conceptually and formally. Something, somewhere, can be seen – maybe here, maybe there – but there is no way of telling what or where it is (MS 5885/1).

The fact that Suzanne wrote has received infelicitous treatment in Beckett studies. Cohn's interpretations have had an enduring impact since she was the person who republished 'F–' (Cohn, 1998). Bair's portrayal of Suzanne as 'the professional musician' who 'had always fancied herself a writer as well' was also extraordinarily callous (Bair, 1978, 580). In any case, the old argument that Suzanne could not have been the author of 'F–' and the 'Petit Sot' poems because she was not known to have written literary texts is now superseded. The refusal to acknowledge her as someone who could write and publish has had other effects, not least that of negating or diminishing her contributions to

Beckett's work. The stories that underlie Suzanne's writing are, of course, part of a wider history of withdrawal, postponement and silence around women, whose documentation remains an arduous process. Some of Josette Hayden's comments are useful to bear in mind here. 'On reste tranquille dans son coin' ('One stays quiet in one's little corner'), she observed in a documentary by Francesca Ragusa that foregrounds her own writings and paintings. Both Hayden and Beckett, she said, sometimes encouraged her to paint more: 'Pourquoi tu travailles pas plus? [...] Mais c'est très bien ce que tu fais là. Pourquoi tu fais pas une exposition?' ('Why are you not doing more work? [...] That's very good, what you're doing. Why don't you do an exhibition?') (*Avec toi sans toi*, 2011). But domestic demands left no space or time for that; she felt under pressure to 'be careful' around Hayden and to spare him any domestic strain; it had also been drilled into her early on that she should not aim above her station as a 'jeune gourde', as Hayden's young and seemingly naïve wife (*Avec toi sans toi*, 2011). It seems likely that Suzanne felt similar pressure; that, as with her musical pursuits, she could only dedicate just about enough time to her writing to keep going on her own.

## 5 The Quiet Work of Suzanne Beckett

In his memoir, Barney Rosset depicts Suzanne as Beckett's 'manager and practical organizer, tending to his every need, protecting him from the world, and vigorously promoting his career' (Rosset, 2016, 123). Considered against the wider spectrum of commentary on Suzanne, this may seem a generous assessment, but it falls short of the truth: indeed, Suzanne also had a direct involvement with Beckett's writing in French and would advise at different stages on the registers of language, aesthetics and rhythm (no small matters with a body of work like Beckett's). This section seeks to account for Suzanne's input on this and other fronts – without trying to hide the difficulties inherent in finding and identifying its sporadic traces, and by allowing space to imagine how nuanced, wide-ranging and crucial her contributions were. That this was informal work makes it no less fundamental; that it was motivated by love and faith in Beckett's talent makes it no less substantial. We should add to this Suzanne's emotional labour to steer Beckett through wavering states of mind and creative impasses, and all the domestic, social and professional arrangements she made to allow him to write undisturbed. The solicitude with which she warned the writer and translator Luce Moreau-Arrabal, Fernando Arrabal's wife, of the ordeals to come should be thought of in this context. '[O]f course it's going to be tough for you, you will have to give many lessons at the Sorbonne so that your husband may write', she said (Fernández, 2015, 231).

Scattered evidence shows that Suzanne's opinion often formed an integral part of Beckett's writing process in French. Pinget noted, for example, that he, Suzanne and Lindon were the first readers of *Comment c'est*, and that Suzanne's input was sought for the titles of *La Manivelle* and *Comment c'est* (MS5519/1/1, 30, 39). As regards Suzanne's input into Beckett's French texts, there are two conclusive sources, both held in the Special Collections of Washington University in St Louis: a typescript of *Mercier et Camier* and a typescript of *Oh les beaux jours*, which are unambiguously annotated in Suzanne's hand. Her annotations to *Mercier et Camier* (in the same neat handwriting she used in her typescripts) are minor but in tune with the spirit of Beckett's text (MS VMF-vmf249). Some corrections pertain to tenses, others to fluency of expression (the accents added throughout are probably in her hand too: the text seems to have been typed on a qwerty typewriter). Some annotations introduce additional humour. This typescript is important because Suzanne's contribution to *Mercier et Camier* – a novel concerned with war and collaboration – has been previously depicted as consisting purely of verbal suggestions while Beckett was writing (Knowlson, 1996, 361). In the Washington University typescript of *Oh les beaux jours*, Suzanne's hand is present throughout and her handwriting is often entangled with Beckett's, with traces in the margins of a live dialogue on word choice and rhythm (MS 008, series 2, box 3, folder 54). Here, too, her suggestions show an acute sense of context and of the registers of language, a profound attention to rhythm and a taste for uncommon expressions and phrases, often quaint, often tinged with generational specificity. From the precise wording to be used for Winnie's hat to terms of endearment, nothing escapes her vigilance. She suggests alternatives and if one of her suggestions has to do with suppressing linguistic colour, she makes another recommendation that adds colour elsewhere. Her suggestions, interestingly, pertain as much to the stage directions, their clarity and evocativeness, as to the words uttered by Winnie and Willie. The working methods revealed in these two typescripts raise an important question: which marks and annotations are hers elsewhere in the archived documents?

This question will remain difficult to answer; goodwill and the naked eye may not suffice. The obstacles will, by now, be familiar. Beckett's correspondence is rarely loquacious about Suzanne, so we cannot turn to his letters for insights. In archived drafts, distinguishing between marginalia in his hand and in her hand can be an uncertain and delicate task, especially when the purpose of the annotation is to be legible. Beckett's handwriting could change sharply from one occasion to the next – Josette Hayden, for example, could discern his mood from the shape of his handwriting on the envelope (*Avec toi sans toi*, 2011) – and his way of tracing letters varied depending on the level of readability needed, with elements of his 'younger', pre-war handwriting sometimes resurfacing unpredictably in his 'older' handwriting. Additionally, he had a whole range of interlocutors – most of them women – as part of his search for *le mot juste* (Bray, too, played an important role later; Sardin, 2024b, 185–94). Some French typescripts feature writing in different, sometimes unidentifiable hands. Sometimes there is a chorus of suggestions: in a truncated typescript of *Molloy* heavily annotated by Mania Péron, some suggestions in grey pencil pertaining to flow, rhythm and character seem to be Suzanne's (Beckett, 2016b, MS-HRC-SB-17–6, f. 214 r, 217 r). Much suggests that Péron – widely recognised as one of Beckett's key editors – was more critical. Suzanne seems to have been more intuitive, to have inhabited the flow, logic and rhythm of Beckett's writing more, and to have been more accepting of idiosyncrasies and more likely to suggest colourful idiomatic expressions. Her open-mindedness, along with her inimitable feel for language, made her a remarkably imaginative and resourceful editor.

Elsewhere, we can discern Suzanne's hand behind several crosswords: in a copybook of *Molloy*, in another containing material from *Watt* and *Malone meurt*, and in the copybook of *L'Expulsé* (inside back cover, HRHRC). These crosswords do not seem to have been copied from a newspaper or magazine but suggest an enthusiasm for 'mots-croisés radiophoniques' or radiophonic crosswords, which required listeners to draw a grid and write down clues dictated by a radio speaker (this type of broadcast became established in the late 1920s on Radio-Paris and endured during and after the war). Suzanne's handwriting can look rushed: that she was writing to dictation is likely. Doing crosswords seems to have been a common pastime, but Suzanne especially liked crosswords, always (JEK/A/7/28), probably because of their formal economy and suggestiveness, and because she was fond of puns, particularly puns that can be made impromptu, that come from everyday language (AMC). The location of the grids in relation to the progress of Beckett's handwritten prose varies. One crossword at the end of the second *Molloy* notebook predates Beckett getting to that page, since he then carefully avoided the ink showing through the paper while writing (Beckett, 2016b, MS-HRC-SB-4–6, 143v-144r). Another appears just before Beckett's drafts of a biographical blurb and a letter requesting an estimate for electrical work at Ralph Cusack's house in Menton (Beckett, 2016b, MS-HRC-SB-4–6, 143r, 144v). At least one crossword appearing in the closing part of *Watt* is simultaneous with the writing, embedded in it; here and elsewhere, the numbering of the grid seems to be in Beckett's hand and the clues are in Suzanne's hand (Beckett, 2017, MS-HRC-SB-7–2, 2r, 13v, 22v, 27v, 45v). It is harder to see who filled in the grids because the capitals are neatly traced, but Beckett's hand seems strongly present. These are not simply charming moments when life shines through but precious reminders of the sharing – of ideas, words, space and time – that happened behind the wall of writing.

In a key domain, the theatre, Suzanne's work is easier to apprehend, not least because Beckett's correspondence sometimes records it. It is well known that she acted as his envoy in theatres performing his plays in France and abroad (he did not attend public performances of his plays after rehearsals and only occasionally went to the theatre). She had a sharp understanding of scenography and acting and remained an important intermediary with actors and theatre directors. Anne-Marie Colombard, who witnessed one of her conversations about stage design with Matias, recalls that she knew exactly what Beckett did and did not want; she would relay this information tactfully and delicately. She knew what he expected because they were in symbiosis for such things, and Beckett had unlimited faith in her (AMC). The mentions of tasks devolved to her in Beckett's letters are brief but crucial. During the rehearsals of *En attendant Godot* at the Théâtre de Babylone, she was sent to check that Estragon's trousers were falling down as expected at the end of Act Two; her comments prompted Beckett to ask Blin to ensure that Pierre Latour would conform to his stage directions, in the first of a long series of similar letters to others (Beckett, 2011, 349). Her priorities remained the quality of scenography and acting, as revealed in her comments on Mihalovici's *Krapp* opera and productions of *Glückliche Tage* relayed in Beckett's correspondence. 'Suzanne went and thought Dooley remarkable', Beckett reported to MacGreevy, 'but a characteristically frightful German mise en scène' (Beckett, 2011, 12). To Alan Schneider, he wrote: 'Suzanne is just back from a few days in Germany where she saw the premiere of H.D. at Düsseldorf and then the Cologne production. Neither of them right, but good acting (Wimmer and Mosheim) and great consciousness and care' (Harmon, 1998, 116). Suzanne's response to Deryk Mendel's approach to *Spiel* enabled Beckett to tell Schneider what to avoid: 'Suzanne did not feel much speed and said there was little visible beam [. . .]. Suzanne found the faces excessively made up and characterized: aging missus and exciting mistress, etc. This would be completely wrong' (Beckett, 2014, 584). We also know from Beckett's letters that Suzanne was one of his trusted sources of advice for *Film*: she, Barney and Christina Rosset, André Hodeir and an unnamed 'movieola girl' were the first people to watch it in two successive groups (Beckett, 2014, 631).

To see productions of Beckett's plays, Suzanne travelled far and wide, to Bielefeld, Berlin, Vienna, Trieste, Venise, Prague, London and Turin notably, with friends such as Marthe Gautier, Denise Deleutre and Madeleine Renaud (Knowlson, 1996, 509; JEK/A/7/24; JEK/A/7/28). With her niece Wanda, Andrée's daughter, she travelled to Turin and Berlin (MTW); with her great-niece Anne-Marie, to Berlin and London (AMC). She seems to have witnessed a considerable number of productions of *Happy Days* in different languages. Trips abroad also provided a respite when the atmosphere around Beckett became too heavy, Gautier suggested (JEK/A/7/28). In Paris, she inhabited the theatre world in ways that Beckett did not; she maintained good relations with key collaborators and honoured invitations, particularly when they came from Roger Blin (declining, as Beckett tended to do, would have eroded goodwill and friendships). She went out to scout talent: she was the person who 'discovered' Deryl Mendel (Knowlson, 1996, 418) and Pierre Chabert. She saw Chabert perform as Krapp in a small Parisian theatre long before he worked with Beckett and initially thought of him as a good actor for Pinget's plays; she reportedly said to Pinget: 'N'est-ce pas, Robert, que Pierre Chabert ferait un excellent interprète pour *L'Hypothèse*?' ('Robert, wouldn't Pierre Chabert make an excellent actor for *L'Hypothèse*?') (Chabert, 2005, 27). With productions of Beckett's plays, she was patient and interested. When the work was not by Beckett and she disliked the approach, she sometimes lost patience. She walked out of the Berliner Ensemble's performance of *Arturo Ui* at the Théâtre des Nations, Beckett reported (Beckett, 2011, 340). Catherine Robbe-Grillet saw her walk out of Henri Pichette's show *Guerre et Poésie* after ten minutes, which she felt was excessive although she, too, found it too long and boring (Robbe-Grillet, 2004, 395).

Much shows that Suzanne preferred the makers to the managers; those who made Beckett's writing live, especially in the theatre, to those who made a living from it as part of a business (publishers like Rosset and Calder had no traction with her). Lindon – the most hands-on of publishers, who could debate the placement of commas for hours (Echenoz, 2001, 51–2) – was in the former category, along with theatre directors and actors. To Schneider, Suzanne wrote a warm letter saying that she would never forget him (MS 1994–34). With Whitelaw, there was no meeting, although Suzanne travelled to London to see her perform at the Royal Court theatre; Suzanne 'was too shy to come up and visit me', Whitelaw concluded (Whitelaw, 1995, 128). Instead, she left a note assuring Whitelaw of her deep esteem (BW B/2). She wrote kind messages of support to the wife of Georges Adet, the actor who had played Nagg in *Fin de Partie*, at a difficult time (Fourcade, 2016, 20). Wherever she saw dedicated hard work, she honoured it in her own way. During one of her Berlin trips, for example, she signified her respect to actors with a nod of the head: it was visible that she was deeply moved, but nothing was said (AMC).

The evidence available also reveals the degree to which Suzanne remained the practical half in the relationship. She had little choice: according to Lindon, Beckett relied on others for simple administrative tasks and could be surprisingly defenceless and naïve when faced with ordinary life demands; Suzanne was, Lindon affirmed, extremely useful to him all along (JEK/A/7/47). Pinget, for his part, wondered what would have become of *En attendant Godot* and the post-war novels without her (Renouard, 1993, 242). Nothing, was Suzanne's opinion: when she discussed this moment in her life, she related her overwhelming sense that, had she not taken matters in hand, Beckett would have continued to write, unread, unpublished, forgotten (AMC). Others helped too, of course, particularly Lindon and Con Leventhal. But Suzanne provided hands-on help for a very long time, Martin recalled (JEK/A/7/53). Her presence was key when Beckett was unwell. She would cancel his appointments, including during the 1970s (Bair, 2020, 32), arrange breathing space when he needed to rest and organise regular holidays until the early 1980s. The least pleasant of the tasks devolved to her was probably letting friends know when they had infringed Beckett's privacy or his perception of the integrity of his work. Cioran was made to understand how much Beckett disliked his article for *Le Monde* on the day of its publication; he resolved never to write for a newspaper again (Cioran, 1997, 810; this was 'Beckett, ou l'horreur d'être né'; 'Beckett, or the horror of being born'). Suzanne was also tasked with informing Pinget that he had caused offense by suggesting that Beckett was actually pleased to feature on the cover of *L'Express* (MS 5519/1/1, 13). Similar tensions arose with the Salzmans over *En attendant Godot* in 1953, when they suggested that its success was a good thing in a gentle attempt to soothe nerves (CS). The friendship with Beckett cooled and ended after that (CS), although Suzanne seems to have continued visiting Ruth (JEK/A/7/53). All this informal work came at a cost, then, although Suzanne was clearly happy to do it.

Things changed when Suzanne turned eighty and her health began to decline. She had been known for her thoughtful and caring nature, but her temperament shifted: she started to act very differently and would put herself first, according to Fournier (JEK/A/7/27). The trigger may have been a growing sense that life was passing by, but it is worth noting that the French translation of Bair's biography appeared around then, in 1979. There had been another sharp turn earlier, in 1969, with Beckett's Nobel Prize. Lindon recalled that Suzanne's personality visibly changed then; she seems to have feared that she was disappearing, because when anyone showed interest in her it was always as Beckett's wife (JEK/A/7/47). According to Annette Lindon, Suzanne became acutely aware that anyone who approached her just wanted to get closer to Beckett – which was indeed the case most of the time, she conceded (JEK/A/7/48). With the Nobel Prize, Fournier pointed out, Suzanne also lost the capacity to fulfil the mission she had set for herself: to enable Beckett to write unhindered (JEK/A/7/27). She is remembered for her response – 'Quelle catastrophe' – but there is more nuance to that than is commonly acknowledged. The Nobel Prize was beginning to be seen as the death knell for a writer's career, as Hannah Simpson notes (Simpson, 2018, 341). Cioran – who often wondered whether obscurity was a blessing or a curse – also described Beckett's prize as a disaster; more precisely, as sheer humiliation for a man as proud as Beckett, who did not want to be understood in the conventional sense (Cioran, 1997, 753). Suzanne's solution, it seems, was to inject very dry humour into the situation. To Blin and Karagheuz, she compared the days spent hiding in their Nabeul hotel, assaulted by journalists, to the situation of the Santé prisoners next to their Paris flat (3 November 1969, IMEC). Later, to her family, she would describe the Nobel Prize as a real nuisance, referring to 'cette tuile qui nous est tombée dessus' (AMC).

Suzanne's concerns about the impact of the Nobel Prize were concrete. She worried about Beckett becoming a magnet for time-wasters (JEK/A/7/8; Cioran, 1997, 825) and often lamented his tendency to agree to all things and meet anyone who asked (AMC; JEK/A/7/27). This was no small matter: Beckett had, Knowlson writes, 'literally, hundreds of friends or acquaintances, from many professions and many countries – painters, musicians, directors, writers, academics – and a surprising number of really close friends' who all expected to see him (Knowlson and Haynes, 2003, 3). The steps the Becketts took to mitigate intrusions at home are well known, particularly the telephone arrangements. Meetings were moved to Montparnasse cafés such as La Closerie des Lilas, La Coupole, Le Dôme or Le Select, and then, as the decades went by, the less glamorous PLM Saint-Jacques across the street. But intrusions remained a fact of life, so much so that a doorbell code known only to family and the closest friends became necessary: one had to ring four times, successively (AMC). On one occasion, an intruder climbed the building to reach their balcony – an incident that Suzanne flatly refused to discuss, but which must have been terrifying. 'Ah non, toi – pas ça' ('Not that – not you') she said to Anne-Marie Colombard with a smile when she asked about it (AMC). From her time on Boulevard Saint-Jacques, Fournier retained vivid memories of journalists ringing the doorbell and demanding photographs with Mr Beckett in ways that seem to have been at best annoying and at worst scary (JEK/A/7/27). Seen from that perspective, there was nothing glamorous or pleasant about fame, and it is no wonder that Suzanne had no interest in stepping out of the shadows.

## 6 Portraits in Different Shades

The grace with which Bettina Jonic summarises the relationship between Beckett and Suzanne – they 'were apart and never left each other's side' (Jonic, 2010) – stands out. Indeed, the biographical literature has few positive things to say, although their bond has attracted much speculation and fascination. Overall, Suzanne has been severely judged, sometimes implicitly deemed responsible for all failings, although Beckett was notoriously unsteady of character and mood and notoriously unfaithful to her. As Nathalie Léger points out, her very name is synonymous with rumours and a long list of reproaches (Léger, 2006, 88–9). This closing section brings together portraits of Suzanne by people who knew her well and less well, drawing attention to the sharp differences between 'la Beckett' (that one-dimensional creature Suzanne never wanted to become) in widely disseminated publications about Beckett and the Suzanne remembered by her friends and relatives.

Friends of Beckett's have made their feelings about Suzanne known; in memoirs celebrating friendships with Beckett, Barney Rosset, John Calder and Anne Atik were especially vocal. In their portraits, Suzanne emerges as someone who does not make good wife material: she is not compliant enough; she grumbles too much, they say. That she did not drink is presented as evidence of her austere personality (Atik, 2001, 20; Calder, 2001, 327) (in reality, she sometimes drank small quantities of white wine, according to Martin, and she once let Fournier understand that she had witnessed as a child the damage that alcoholism can do; JEK/A/7/53; JEK/A/7/27). The facts levelled against her when she was in her late fifties and early sixties are desperately ordinary: she has no interest in going on drinking sprees; she resents poorly chosen presents and impolite or thoughtless behaviour (Atik, 2001, 19; Rosset, 2016, 125). What is noteworthy is how these published accounts clash with Rosset's, Calder's and Atik and Arikha's private interviews with Knowlson during the making of *Damned to Fame*. These earlier discussions are more even-handed and shed a different light on Suzanne – as someone who did not forgive social naivety and social gaffes (JEK/1/7/4), who was keen to take work and worry off Beckett's shoulders (JEK/A/7/18) and who grew weary of being excluded from conversations (JEK/A/7/69). That there were linguistic and cultural barriers is certain: Suzanne did not hide when Charles Juliet – Beckett's only French memoirist with André Bernold – visited, and she was cordial (Juliet, 1999, 13, 61). The wordings used by Rosset and Atik reveal an expectation that Suzanne ought to have spoken English to them. Atik was then beginning to learn French (Atik, 2001, 20), while Rosset's French was approximative enough for him to think of Paris intra-muros as 'the *banlieu*' [sic] or *banlieue* – the suburbs further away, beyond the *périphérique* (Rosset, 2009, 20; Rosset, 2016, 125). Rosset, the only one who seems to have mourned his friendship with Suzanne (JEK/A/7/69), went as far as speculating that Suzanne disliked Americans (*Waiting for Beckett*, 1993). It is more likely that she lost patience with the conversational patterns that developed around her as the only French speaker and that she found being ignored very rude (JEK/A/7/18; see also Atik, 2001, 20; Jonic, 2010).

Impressions garnered in passing by others who did not make claims to authority are more nuanced. Relating a one-off encounter with Suzanne in *The Observer*, Frank Delaney described 'a strong personality, with whom received opinion, I guessed, gained no ground. No trace in her face of a woman married to the most depressed man in Europe. [...] The impression that remains is of a sharp, defended woman, with a high personal culture, a quick elegance and excellent manners' (Delaney, 1996, 4). His portrait accords with that offered by Jonic, who knew Suzanne a little more (they met five times). Jonic (who has the honesty of admitting to a brief affair with Beckett too) describes Suzanne as someone who disliked immature or careless behaviour and got bored by drunken antics and lewd conversation disguised as bohemianism (Jonic, 2010). The contrast with Calder's account is stark: Calder, Jonic's former husband, portrays Suzanne as a troublemaker determined to prevent Beckett from having a good time – like Bray, said to 'nag' (Calder, 2001, 326). Calder's world was not congenial to women: Jonic sketches out a stultifying environment ruled by 'bad manners, lapsed morals and forgotten responsibilities' where she often feared she might become a 'squashed centipede' (Jonic, 2010). Some recollections elsewhere of conversations with and around Beckett come across poorly today; whether Beckett's propensity to make racy jokes made the women around laugh as much as the men, for example, seems unlikely (Horovitz, 1997, 189; Walker, 2014, 6; see also MS 5519/1/1, 16, 44). Such anecdotes are all too ordinary and, of course, this is not the kind of climate that leaves hard, universally legible evidence; acknowledging its existence, however, is important.

If we want better-rounded, less anecdotal portraits of Suzanne, we must look elsewhere, at recollections of friends and relatives that are largely unpublished. What unites accounts from Suzanne's friends is the warmth with which they recalled her talent for friendship. Fandos remembered her as a 'charming' person and 'the best friend I've ever had' (Fandos, 2024). Likewise, Pinget described her as a perfect friend in his diary (MS 5519/1/167, 67). His dedication in a copy of *Le Renard et la boussole* celebrates a privileged bond: 'Pour Suzanne/ avec ma vieille, ma [seule],/ et inarrachable amitié' ('For Suzanne, with my old friendship, that unique and untearable bond') (Van Hulle, Nixon and Neyt, 2016). Elsewhere, he acknowledges her as 'an adorable woman' characterised by her solicitude, warmth and devotion to Beckett and her friends (Renouard, 1993, 242). Implicit here is the contrast with Beckett, whom Pinget finds too self-absorbed, prone to repeating the same things, sometimes disturbingly disconnected from his surroundings, to the point where serving olive oil instead of whisky seemed of no consequence (MS 5519/1/1, 66–8). Cioran's *Cahiers* follow a similar path: the moments spent in Beckett's company are life-changing, but also sometimes upsetting, and he struggles to approach him: Beckett does not do conversation, he says (Cioran, 1997, 613). Suzanne becomes the interlocutor who evens things out, with whom pleasant moments are spent (Cioran, 1997, 825, 996). Arrabal, too, saw 'Mademoiselle Suzanne' as someone who was just as fascinating, if not more fascinating, than Beckett and was struck by her elegance and integrity (Arrabal, 1993, 25; Fernández, 2015).

In other contexts, the qualities most often evoked are Suzanne's profound kindness, generosity, sense of humour, loyalty and attentiveness. Mita Tuby kept fond memories of Suzanne's personality many decades after they lost touch (JEK/C/1/149). Denise Deleutre defined her as a faithful and kind friend (JEK/A/7/24); Martin as someone who had many friends and with whom relations were simple (JEK/A/7/53); Chiarini as a great listener interested in things big and small, whose responses were heartfelt (JEK/A/7/19); Karagheuz as an independent woman who had a well-balanced life and liked nothing more than going out and having a good laugh (JEK/A/7/42). Michèle Meunier felt that her finesse was her most striking characteristic (JEK/A/7/59). Likewise, Suzanne's great-niece Anne-Marie Colombard has vivid memories of her as someone who understood things immediately, intuitively, with unusual depth and accuracy. Suzanne was a quick judge of situations and could discern nuances in behaviour and dynamics that would have been imperceptible to many others (AMC). Even in her late eighties, when she became very unwell, she could guess instantly whether the people she cared for were happy or not, before they had spoken (AMC). Like Beckett, she would listen intently when she asked people how they were; if anything was wrong, she would sympathise in a genuine, heart-warming way (AMC). Like Beckett, she could not stand the thought of anyone suffering (AMC). She had deep admiration for the people she met in daily life who kept going in the face of adversity, from elderly women pulling their trolley alone to homeless men on the street (AMC). She encouraged artistic and intellectual initiative, no matter how small, from learning to play an instrument to getting to grips with a new academic subject: 'Lance-toi' ('Just do it') was her recommendation to Anne-Marie (AMC).

For Michèle Tholozan-Warluzel, what characterises Suzanne's outlook on life is her commitment to the vanguard, revealed not simply in her interest in artists and writers who were younger than her but in her dedication to healthy living at a time when there was no such culture (MTW). As Beckett put it, Suzanne would '[take] care of herself' (Beckett, 2011, 640), and her ways of doing so were in keeping with common concerns today. She practised yoga every day and had an interest in vegetarianism and macrobiotics – an approach moderated, of course, by her love of cigarettes and Montparnasse restaurants (AMC; MTW; JEK/A/7/59; JEK/A/7/47). She frequented the few organic and health food shops that existed in Paris then; her friend Denise, Roger Deleutre's wife, ran such a shop and sold imported German products such as *Vollkornbrot* (AMC). In other regards, Suzanne was firmly of her generation, particularly when it came to making do with little. Her use of alternative medicine has been routinely depicted as bizarre, if not horrifying, by anglophone scholars, but it was also a generational trait: many people her age in France, who had survived the war and sometimes severe disease with little or no access to medical care, turned to such remedies in an attempt to preserve their natural immunity, the war having taught them that basic medication can suddenly vanish.

There were other sides to Suzanne's personality, which were less traditionally feminine and are all the more interesting for it. Her way of expressing herself was very much her own: she had a remarkable gift for minimalist statements and could express things of great profundity, including her satisfaction or frustration, in strikingly few words (AMC). She could be very cutting, she commanded respect, she was sharp (MTW; AMC; see also JEK/A/7/27; JEK/A/7/8; Tholozan-Warluzel, 2024, 155). Mathieu Lindon credits her for a helpful lesson in understanding human foibles around money and for some of Beckett's colourful expletives: the expression 'foutre tant pis' (an unusual variation around 'doesn't fucking matter') used by Beckett was hers, he states (Lindon, 2023, 69; see also Beckett, 2016a, 672).[8] She certainly enjoyed being irreverent (MS 5519/1/1, 41, 44). She could be deeply eccentric, Annette Lindon said to Knowlson, in an often spiteful interview showing that the real friendship was between her husband and Suzanne (JEK/A/7/48). She seems to have seized the opportunity to behave in uncharacteristic ways when she could. Marthe Gautier remembered how, during a trip to Germany in February 1961, she and Suzanne asked Matias to take them to the Reeperbahn; they were curious to see it but would not have gone there alone (JEK/A/7/28). She dressed in exactly the way she liked and liked to alter clothes (Tholozan-Warluzel, 2024, 153), sometimes assembling different garments from Parisian flea markets to make something new (AMC). She stayed barefoot in her shoes, always made of fine suede, in all temperatures (AMC) – a relic of the war years, probably, when stockings were as rare as gold dust. She wouldn't give away her age and left it up to her tombstone to indicate it (AMC).

---

[8] '[A] remark made by Suzanne, Beckett's wife, is still useful to me. She claimed, to summarise the conversation, that when someone says, "Guess how much I paid for such and such", one ought to respond by doubling one's estimate, whereas one ought to reduce one's estimate by half in response to "Guess how much I sold such and such for"' (Lindon, 2023, 161).

When it came to domestic life, she seems to have both embraced and despised constraints. Martin and Josette Hayden remembered her as obsessed with cleanliness and tidiness (JEK/A/7/53; JEK/A/7/33); Michèle Tholozan-Warluzel as someone who had no interest in being a homemaker (Tholozan-Warluzel, 2024, 154). In her late seventies, when it became necessary to employ someone to help with housework, she found an *homme de ménage* and made a point of referring to him as such (JEK/A/7/24; AMC) (*femme de ménage* is a consecrated French phrase whose gendering does not normally budge). She left it up to the Lindons and others to host dinner parties; when entertaining friends, she made simple meals and preferred going to restaurants. Martin reported that she cooked often (JEK/A/7/53). Denise Deleutre remembered her lack of interest in cooking (JEK/A/7/24), and so did Arikha, who attributed it to Suzanne's feminism (JEK/1/7/4). Annette Lindon, who lived nearby on Boulevard Arago, would see the elderly Suzanne buy ready-made salads and perceived such shortcuts as a serious domestic failure (JEK/A/7/48). Her husband Jérôme was especially aware that the harsh judgements imposed upon Suzanne had to do with her dislike of domestic constraints (JEK/A/7/48). This is a pertinent observation, given how Suzanne's refusal to conform to the role of obedient wife tends to transform her into a problematic figure in biographical writing on Beckett that claims privileged insights into his thoughts and character.

The more Suzanne aged, the less she became willing to be self-effacing and pliable, and the more she expressed her scepticism towards social conventions. She found common language traits and social habits increasingly difficult to bear, especially the idea that anyone could claim ownership over anyone else. 'Ma soeur, pourquoi "ma"?' ('My sister – why "my"?') she would ask disapprovingly (AMC). She found a story Pinget had told her, about a woman who introduces her husband to a friend and cannot help but laugh when she utters the words 'mon mari' (MS 5519/1/1, 41), irrepressibly funny. Although she remained devoted to her family, she wanted to be surrounded by people she had chosen herself (AMC) and would jokingly refer to her friends as family (MS 5519/1/1, 66). We can relate her contempt for the institution of marriage to her keen sense of social absurdity. When she married Beckett in 1961 to secure her testamentary rights, she was not enthused by the arrangement: the marriage had been decided, she said to her nephew Yvan, 'pour des raisons administratives', for administrative reasons (AMC). As the phrase 'pour des raisons administratives' commonly involves justifying some sort of inconvenience (a closure, an eroded service, a delay, generally announced after the facts), there is humour behind that phrasing, as well as evident suffering. 'For administrative reasons' seems a reasonable summary of a situation which she felt had become ridiculous (JEK/A/7/53).

About Beckett's affairs Suzanne was no fool. But when she confided to friends, she did not linger on her feelings (JEK/A/7/48; JEK/A/7/53). Her most explicit warning was to Pinget, in 1960: she told him that becoming attached to Beckett would only bring disappointment (MS 5519/1/1, 45). Annette Lindon was probably right when she described Suzanne as someone who had experienced profound boredom and suffering (JEK/A/7/48). Meunier, too, remembered Suzanne's unhappiness, as well as her desire to make do and defend her ground (JEK/A/7/59). Perhaps infidelity had been part of the picture for longer than we imagine: it seems that Beckett was unfaithful to her years before the affairs that are already known (Beckett to Duthuit, Ussy Thursday [1949], DUTH6; JEK/1/7/4). Much could be written about the pain caused by arrangements made sotto voce or left unspoken in this milieu: the double life that Jérôme Lindon, for example, led with the writer and journalist Madeleine Chapsal (a key figure at the magazine *L'Express*) is common knowledge; the relationship started to wind down when Chapsal realised that she was losing the will to live (Chapsal, 2018, 335). Bray, who moved from England to Paris just before the Becketts' marriage, seemed terribly unhappy to Jonic whenever she met her (Jonic, 2010). Beckett did compartmentalise his life, but sometimes his vigilance lapsed (Knowlson, 1996, 554). We can see this in the list of twelve select guests he drew for the final dress rehearsal of *Fin de partie* at the TEP (Théâtre de l'Est Parisien) in October 1980 – an event that Suzanne may well have attended. Gautier was invited and so was Bray (Correspondance 1980–1, IMEC).

What is certain is that behind each report of Suzanne refusing to comply with expectations there is another story. The layout of the flat on Boulevard Saint-Jacques is a good example: according to Martin, Suzanne wanted her own space because she was deeply committed to her writing (JEK/A/7/53). Living arrangements such as those of Monique Haas and Marcel Mihalovici, who worked harmoniously side by side in the smallest of flats, had probably become impossible for her and Beckett by that stage. Suzanne's avoidance of Ussy-sur-Marne is another good example. She took to the village with enthusiasm at first, but visited less often after 1957 and decided that she would never set foot there again sometime before 1967 (Knowlson, 1996, 441, 546). To Jonic, Beckett said that Suzanne had 'retreated' because the Haydens were living close by (Jonic, 2010). To Knowlson, Martin related how Josette Hayden had fallen head over heels for Beckett and how glaringly obvious this was to everyone around (JEK/A/7/53; JEK/A/7/18). The interviews and documents featured in Ragusa's documentary *Avec toi sans toi* revolve around the affair that took place at some point; Josette wrote about it in her notebooks but never admitted to it verbatim. That situation must have represented a terrible betrayal for Suzanne, since Josette had been her confidante, Cronin tells us, on intimate matters including the choice of not having children (Cronin, [1996] 1997, 368).

When Beckett spoke about his marriage to Lawrence Shainberg, he affirmed that there had been 'many near-ruptures, as a matter of fact'; he suggested that having his 'own door' had helped and 'seemed rather pleased with his marriage, extremely grateful that it had lasted' (Shainberg, [1987] 1992, 25). Suzanne was more discreet, even with friends. The only direct traces of her dissatisfaction feature in Pinget's diary: an entry from 1961 records Suzanne complaining of Beckett's unpleasantness and abruptness and reports a deliberate attempt from him to be hurtful (MS 5519/1/1, 68). An earlier entry portrays Beckett as someone who needed constant supervision with simple everyday tasks when he was at a low ebb and gives a sense of Suzanne's patience (MS 5519/1/1, 45). In separate interviews with Knowlson, the Lindons spoke of the ferocity with which Beckett would look at Suzanne; Annette felt that this was unavoidable in any long marriage (JEK/A/7/48), but Jérôme seemed troubled by the manner in which Beckett would freeze and seem consumed with rage when Suzanne tried to fill his silences or made attempts at small talk (JEK/A/7/47). It is well known that Beckett's drinking worried Suzanne; on the nature of his drinking and her worry the sources diverge, however. While the dominant trend has been to present his drinking affectionately, in a boys-will-be-boys mode, those who knew Suzanne well expressed different views. Edward Beckett felt that her concern was normal and her ways of expressing it were legitimate (JEK/A/7/8). Meunier found her very tolerant, noting that there was nothing anyone could do about alcoholism when it was embedded (JEK/A/7/59). Fournier spoke about her resignation too and observed that Beckett's way of drinking with rapid, stiff gestures denoted a real addiction (JEK/A/7/27).

The more successful Beckett became, the more Suzanne sought refuge in her friendships. They had common friends – the Salzmans and the Duthuits in the 1940s and early 1950s, the Lindons and the Mihalovicis thereafter, Arikha before his relationship with Anne Atik, Pinget and Cioran (Simone Boué was not included in their evenings with Cioran). Suzanne was fond of Thomas MacGreevy but otherwise seems to have kept at a distance from Beckett's own friends. She enjoyed lively conversation, which caused tension sometimes. The silences of the Van Velde brothers, for example, were a source of irritation once added to Beckett's own, she later recalled, and she preferred to leave when they came to Rue des Favorites (JEK/A/7/27). Strain could come from unpredictable directions: Bram Van Velde, she later confided, had fallen for her and this manifested itself in ways that exerted further pressure on her relationship with Beckett (JEK/A/7/53). This may be what Beckett refers to in a letter to Duthuit complaining that Van Velde has lost his mind and that, if he is still visiting, it is emphatically not to talk about work (Duthuit, Ussy Thursday [1949]). The matter was allegedly resolved when financial hardship ended and the Becketts moved (JEK/A/7/53). In other contexts, making herself invisible remained her strategy. To Georges Belmont, Beckett joked that Suzanne did exist but was difficult to spot (28 December 1951, MS 17.15).[9]

Her own friends were different from Beckett's – more down-to-earth, perhaps, and less in pursuit of recognition. She relished originality wherever she saw it and appreciated atypical people (AMC). The pattern that surfaces from her friendships is her preference for people who disliked the status quo, who lived their lives differently and sometimes suffered for it. It is noteworthy, for example, that she should have developed close friendships with gay men in times of acute homophobia in France. Recent work on Pinget, notably, inscribes his texts into gay and queer studies and examines his parodies of heterosexual society, while also acknowledging his reluctance to publicly discuss his sexuality (Ruffel, 2013). Suzanne's closest female friends rose to high prominence in professions heavily dominated by men; Monique Haas, Madeleine Renaud and Marthe Gautier all received the Légion d'Honneur, France's highest honour, for their achievements in music, theatre and medicine, respectively.[10] Haas, the virtuoso pianist, became one of the stars of Deutsche Grammophon and has left an abundant discography with other leading classical music labels (Beckett's correspondence, which expresses a lack of enthusiasm for Haas's concerts, contrasts sharply with the effusive, unanimous praise that greeted her performances from her international public and from musicians and composers, throughout her career). With Haas, Suzanne shared not simply a love of the piano but an experience of wartime hardship. Haas had spent much of the war in hiding in Cannes and elsewhere in the Provence, and had joined a strand of the intellectual Resistance affiliated to the French Communist Party, then banned. With Gautier, initially a friend of Martin's, Suzanne shared a sympathy for the vulnerable, the displaced, the marginalised, along with a reluctance to linger on the past. Gautier is well known today as a victim of institutional misogyny, thanks to numerous magazine articles, radio and television broadcasts, and a novel – *Ce qui nous revient* by Corinne Royer – that examines her trajectory against the wider erasure of women's contributions to science (Royer, 2019). It is certain that friends were a saving grace for Gautier too, and that she found solace in her outings and travels

---

[9] That she refused to meet Belmont seems likely if she knew of his wartime record in the Vichy government as Georges Pelorson.

[10] Renaud felt that she knew little about Beckett (Renaud, 2000, 51, 79). Based on her wordings, we can conclude that the friendship was with Suzanne.

with Suzanne. In 1958 – probably when their friendship began – Gautier discovered the chromosomal cause of Down's syndrome in the laboratory she had ingeniously set up, then saw her discovery usurped by her two superiors. Whenever she spoke about this time, she described her disgust and feeling of injustice and emphasised that she had no alternative but to stay silent and turn away. She built a new career in leading Paris hospitals and at the French National Institute of Health and Medical Research, INSERM, and became one of the founding figures in paediatric cardiology in France – a fact that seems relevant to *Lessness* and its image of a child's struggling heart.

What is known of Suzanne's life after the move to Boulevard Saint-Jacques shows that she frequented theatres, museums, exhibitions, concert halls and cinemas assiduously. A love of the theatre connected many of her friends. Jean Martin, Roger Blin, Madeleine Renaud, Manolo Fandos, Matias (Charles Henrioud), Nicole Kessel, Michèle Meunier and Hermine Karagheuz worked as actors, directors, stage designers or costume designers. When Suzanne travelled, it was not just to see Beckett's plays: she took regular holidays with Beckett and with friends. With Fandos, Martin and Gautier, for example, she travelled in Spain and to Catalonia; she also visited Fandos in Ibiza (Fandos, 2024). In Paris, she would practise the piano in Gautier's flat on Rue de Douai on Friday afternoons while Gautier was at work (JEK/A/7/24). The offer had been made in the context of a friendship characterised by a mutual respect for privacy (JEK/A/7/28). The walls on Rue des Favorites and Boulevard Saint-Jacques were thin, Gautier recalled, and Suzanne did not want to disturb Beckett or her neighbours (*Samuel Beckett: Silence to Silence*, 1984). Playing alone, uninterrupted, then moving straight to a dinner cooked by Gautier's maid seemed the height of luxury to Suzanne and brought her great relief (JEK/A/7/24; JEK/A/7/27). Many Friday evenings during the 1960s were spent in Gautier's flat with Martin, Fandos, Chiarini and Denise Deleutre (this became the weekly routine between 1965 and 1970). Later, there were regular evenings out with an ever-expanding group that sometimes included relatives of Suzanne's. A typical outing involved going to see a play – at the Odéon-Théâtre de France or, after Barrault's dismissal, the Elysée-Montmartre where Barrault and Renaud had relocated – then a meal at a nearby restaurant (AMC). Chiarini would drive Suzanne home afterwards (AMC). The conversations revolved around their own lives (JEK/A/7/19). These were joyful moments, full of laughter and jokes (AMC). It is difficult to find common ground between this real Suzanne – whose favourite conversational sport, Karagheuz recalls, was making others laugh, especially Beckett (Karagheuz, [2002] 2021, 41; JEK/A/7/42) – and the surly creature portrayed in the biographical literature centred on Beckett.

## 7 Conclusion

To Lindon, Beckett once deplored his inability to demonstrate appreciation and affection to those who mattered the most to him, noting that this character trait would bring him suffering on his day of reckoning (5 January 1963, IMEC). Sometimes, it seems, he wished that life could have turned out differently and this wish expressed itself in peculiar ways, largely mediated through his writing. Without explaining why or how, Bray believed that *Happy Days* and *Play* were about Suzanne (Kędzierski, 2011, 892) – although these plays are hardly compatible with the real Suzanne's dislike of the strictures of femininity and bourgeois pretence (JEK/A/7/42).[11] Bray also remembered encouraging Beckett to write 'something which is a sort of a tribute to Suzanne' – which, she suggests, he failed to do (Kędzierski, 2011, 892). *Ohio Impromptu* may have been that: to Knowlson, Beckett confided that the 'dear face' imagined within it was that of Suzanne and that the play had been spurred by imagining himself 'trudging out to her grave' (Knowlson, 1996, 665). When the macabre fantasy became reality, he was 'sad and filled with remorse', Knowlson reports (703). 'So much regret, so much regret' were his words (666). He talked to Lindon about the profound serenity of Suzanne's face on her deathbed and confessed that he envied her that (JEK/A/7/47). As a last goodbye to her on the day of her burial, he picked a wildflower, probably from cracks in the concrete yard of his care home, and hung onto it until he could lay it on her coffin (JEK/A/7/47).

Suzanne's attachment to Beckett made her vulnerable too, and she seems to have alternately embraced and resented her undying loyalty to him. The last report of her being seen in public, three months before her death, mentions a photography exhibition at the Swedish Embassy in Paris featuring portraits of Beckett (O'Brien, 2016, 62), presumably in celebration of the Nobel Prize. During the last year of her life, she became haunted by a song her grandmother used to sing and by another poem she would try to recreate; when Beckett visited, she would recite fragments to him, in an accusatory fashion it seems (JEK/A/7/27). The lines Edith Fournier saw Suzanne search for belong to two poems that I have been able to trace, which marvel at the ability of love to endure in spite of all. One is Nicolas Boileau's 'Vers à mettre en chant', whose speaker laments his inability to stop loving despite the scale of the betrayal. 'Mon cœur, vous soupirez au nom de l'infidèle/ Avez vous oublié que vous ne l'aimez plus?', the refrain asks ('Oh my heart, you sigh upon the

---

[11] Peter Boxall shows how we can balance the play's autobiographical dimension (with Bray, rather than Suzanne, acting as the major influence) and its politics of togetherness and isolation to understand its transformative philosophy (Boxall, 2024, 291–307).

name of the unfaithful,/ Have you forgotten that your love is long gone?'; Boileau, 1800, 306–7). The other is 'Les deux coeurs' ('The two hearts'), originally a Breton folksong, popularised as a libretto for piano in the 1890s by Cécile Chaminade (a composer Philipp valued). The poem urges two lovers to avoid tearing themselves apart and to respect their pact, and describes their hearts as so entangled that separation without profound suffering is impossible.[12]

We can begin to understand the relationship between Beckett and Suzanne, Nathalie Léger affirms, if we approach it tentatively; if we embrace suggestion and interrogation instead of working with affirmation and categorisation (Léger, 2006, 88–9). In many ways, describing their bond – both extraordinary and deeply ordinary – has become the preserve of novelists, who – untrammeled by copyright permissions and difficulties in gathering and deciphering documents – are freer to imagine and suggest. In the racing thoughts of the elderly Beckett created by Maylis Besserie in *Le Tiers Temps*, Suzanne – intrepid, irreverent, quick-thinking – is acutely missed. The young Suzanne imagined in Jo Baker's *A Country Road, a Tree* is the provider, the maker, Beckett's resourceful guide, confronting the same wartime risks and choices as him. These might be highly fictionalised portraits, but the appetite for freedom that they foreground comes close to the truth. Without doubt, this woman who was so determined, courageous, full of faith in the importance of

---

[12]

    Le cœur que tu m'avais donné,
    Ma douce amie, en gage,
    Ne l'ai perdu ni détourné
    Ni mis à fol usage.
    L'ai mêlé tant et tant au mien,
    Que ne sais plus quel est le tien.

    Pourquoi vouloir les diviser?
    A ce penser je tremble:
    Sans effort pourrait-on briser
    Le nœud qui les rassemble!
    Il faudrait déchirer le mien,
    Hélas! peut-être aussi le tien.
    A les séparer désormais,

    Nous souffririons l'un l'autre;
    Laissons-les unis pour jamais,
    Ce destin est le nôtre.
    Ne cherchons plus quel est le tien,
    Ne cherchons plus quel est le mien.

                                (Lucas, 1893, 1–2)

literature will continue to inspire new thinking. The manner in which she led her life and the singularity of that life will continue to command attention and respect. Rethinking her peculiar absence in the large mass of materials about Beckett is not simply a question of doing justice where justice is due: it also raises profound questions about ways of thinking of literature that leave little space to life, love and the realities of work.

# References

## Interviews

### Interviews with the Author

Anne-Marie Colombard (AMC), 12 April 2024.
Alexandre Dandelot (AD), 6 June 2024.
Marthe Gautier (MG), 7 November 2012.
Claude Salzman (CS), 14 March 2024.
Michèle Tholozan-Warluzel (MTW), 11 and 12 April 2024.

### James and Elizabeth Knowlson Collection, University of Reading, Special Collections

JEK/1/7/4. Interview with Avigdor Arikha. Transcript.
JEK/A/7/8. Interview with Edward Beckett. Transcript.
JEK/A/7/18. Interview with John Calder. Transcript.
JEK/A/7/19. Interview with Alberto Chiarini. Transcript.
JEK/A/7/24. Interview with Denise Deleutre. Transcript.
JEK/A/7/27. Interview with Edith Fournier. Transcript.
JEK/A/7/28. Interview with Marthe Gautier. Transcript.
JEK/A/7/33. Interview with Josette Hayden. Transcript.
JEK/A/7/42. Interview with Hermine Karagheuz. Transcript.
JEK/A/7/47. Interview with Jérôme Lindon. Transcript.
JEK/A/7/48. Interview with Annette Lindon. Transcript.
JEK/A/7/53. Interview with Jean Martin. Transcript.
JEK/A/7/56. Interview with Marysette Mayoux. Transcript.
JEK/A/7/59. Interview with Michèle Meunier. Transcript.
JEK/A/7/61. Interview with Pamela Mitchell. Transcript.
JEK/A/7/67. Interview with Alexis Péron. Transcript.
JEK/A/7/69. Interview with Barney Rosset. Transcript.
JEK/C/1/149. Interview with Mita and Edmund [sic] Tuby.

## Archival Materials

### Bibliothèque Nationale de France

BNF MS-20035. 'Quatre Chansons de Bilitis' by Georges Dandelot.

BNF MS-20007. 'La Belle Yolande (chanson de toile du XIIe siècle), musique de G. Dandelot'.
BOB/28560, R/183615. Letters to Georges Dandelot.
RES/VMC/MS-134 (1 2). Nadia Boulanger's student registers, 1923–4, 1928–9 and 1930–1.

## IMEC (Institut Mémoires de l'édition contemporaine)

Fonds Beckett.
Letters to Roger Blin.

## Bibliothèque Kandinsky, Centre Pompidou

DUTH 6. Correspondence Samuel Beckett–Georges Duthuit, 1947–72.
DUTH 36. *Transition*: Textes divers.
DUTH 38. *Transition*: Correspondance.
DUTH 40. Revue 'Transition 48' no. 4 (1948): Textes préparatoires et maquette.

## University of Reading, Special Collections

BW/B/2. Letter from Suzanne Beckett to Billie Whitelaw.
JEK/A/3/77/13. Resistance – Samuel Beckett.
JEK/A/3/68. Poems Research files II.
JEK/D/1/6. Photographs (Suzanne Beckett (née Deschevaux-Dumesnil)).
MS 5519/1/1. Pinget, Robert, 'Notre ami Samuel Beckett' (1960–1).
MS 5885/1–5. Typescripts by Suzanne Dumesnil.

## Harry Ransom Center, University of Texas at Austin

Letters from Samuel Beckett to John Fletcher.
Letters from Samuel Beckett to Susan Manning.
Manuscript Notebook 2 of *Watt*, box 6.
Manuscript of *L'Expulsé*, box 3, folder 6.
MS 17.15, Carlton Lake Collection. Letters from Samuel Beckett to Georges Belmont.
MS 19.14, Carlton Lake Collection. Beckett, Suzanne, 'J'aurai seize ans aux fleurs nouvelles ...'.

## John J. Burns Library, Boston College

MS 1994-34. Letter from Suzanne Beckett to Alan Schneider, 4 July 1960.

## Special Collections, University of Washington in St Louis

MS VMF-vmf249. Typescript of *Mercier et Camier*.
Typescript of *Oh les beaux jours*. Samuel Beckett Papers, MS 008, series 2, box 3, folder 54.

## Personal Collection of Michèle Tholozan-Warluzel

Déchevaux-Dumesnil family photographs.
Letters from Jeanne Déchevaux-Dumesnil to Andrée Déchevaux-Dumesnil.
Letters from Suzanne Déchevaux-Dumesnil to Andrée Déchevaux-Dumesnil.

## Print and Other Sources

Anzieu, Didier (1992), *Beckett et le psychanalyste*, Paris: Archimbaud.
Arnold, Bruce (1999), 'From Proof to Print: Anthony Cronin's *Samuel Beckett: The Last Modernist* Reconsidered', *Samuel Beckett Today/Aujourd'hui*, 8, pp. 217–19.
Arrabal, Fernando (1993), *Genios y figuras*, Madrid: Espasa Calpe.
Atik, Anne (2001), *How It Was: A Memoir of Samuel Beckett*, London: Faber & Faber.
*Avec toi sans toi*, film, directed by Francesca Ragusa. Paris: La Vie est Belle, 2011.
Bair, Deirdre (1978), *Samuel Beckett: A Biography*, London: Cape.
Bair, Deirdre (2020), *Parisian Lives: Samuel Beckett, Simone de Beauvoir and Me*, London: Atlantic.
Banier, François-Marie (2009), *Beckett*, Göttigen: Steidl.
Beckett, Samuel (2009), *The Letters of Samuel Beckett, Vol. 1: 1929–1940*, ed. Martha Dow Fehsenfeld and Lois More Overbeck, Cambridge: Cambridge University Press.
Beckett, Samuel (2011), *The Letters of Samuel Beckett, Vol. 2: 1941–1956*, ed. George Craig, Martha Dow Fehsenfeld, Dan Gunn and Lois More Overbeck, Cambridge: Cambridge University Press.
Beckett, Samuel (2014), *The Letters of Samuel Beckett, Vol. 3: 1957–1965*, ed. George Craig, Martha Dow Fehsenfeld, Dan Gunn and Lois More Overbeck, Cambridge: Cambridge University Press.
Beckett, Samuel (2016a), *The Letters of Samuel Beckett, Vol. 4: 1966–1989*, ed. George Craig, Martha Dow Fehsenfeld, Dan Gunn and Lois More Overbeck, Cambridge: Cambridge University Press.
Beckett, Samuel (2016b), *Molloy: A Digital Genetic Edition*, ed. Edouard Magessa O'Reilly, Dirk Van Hulle, Pim Verhulst and Vincent Neyt, Brussels: ASP/University Press Antwerp, www.beckettarchive.org

Beckett, Samuel (2017), *Malone meurt/Malone Dies: A Digital Genetic Edition*, ed. Dirk Van Hulle, Pim Verhulst and Vincent Neyt, Brussels: ASP/University Press Antwerp, www.beckettarchive.org.

Berest, Anne and Claire Berest (2017), *Gabriële*, Paris: Stock.

Bernold, André (1992), *L'Amitié de Beckett, 1979–1989*, Paris: Hermann.

Blau, Herbert (2000), *Sails of the Herring Fleet: Essays on Beckett*, Ann Arbor, MI: University of Michigan Press.

Boileau, Nicolas Despréaux (1800), *Œuvres, tome premier*, Paris: Didot.

Boxall, Peter (2024), *The Possibility of Literature: The Novel and the Politics of Form*, Cambridge: Cambridge University Press.

Brater, Enoch (1989), *Why Beckett*, London: Thames & Hudson.

Calder, John (2001), *Pursuit: Uncensored Memoirs*, London: Calder.

Campagne, Jean-Marc (1937), 'New York, Hollywood, Paris, avec Lucien Lelong', *Marianne*, 25 November, p. 13.

Chabert, Pierre (2005), 'L'Auteur, l'auteur, où se trouve l'auteur', in Jean-Marie Thomasseau (ed.), *Le Théâtre au plus près: Pour André Veinstein*, Saint-Denis: Presses Universitaires de Vincennes, pp. 27–42.

Chapsal, Madeleine (2018), *Souvenirs involontaires*, Paris: Fayard.

Charpentier, Raymond (1920), 'L'Enseignement musical: Une intéressante initiative', *Comoedia*, 13 November, p. 1.

Cioran (1997), *Cahiers 1957–1972*, ed. Simone Boué, Paris: Gallimard.

Cohn, Ruby (1998), 'The "F–" Story', *Samuel Beckett Today/Aujourd'hui*, 7, pp. 41–5.

Cohn, Ruby (2001), *A Beckett Canon*, Ann Arbor, MI: University of Michigan Press.

Cosnay, Marie (2006), *Villa Chagrin*, Lagrasse: Verdier.

Cronin, Anthony ([1996] 1997), *Samuel Beckett: The Last Modernist*, London: Flamingo.

Curran, Beverley (2006), 'Review of *Beckett Remembering/Remembering Beckett: A Centenary Celebration* by Elizabeth Knowlson and James Knowlson', *Journal of Irish Studies*, 21, pp. 140–1.

*Dance First*, film, directed by James Marsh. Sky Original, 2023.

Dandelot, Alexandre (2017), 'Georges Dandelot (1895–1975): Vie sociale, vie privée d'un compositeur oublié', dissertation, ENM [Ecole Nationale de Musique, Danse et Art Dramatique] de Villeurbanne, www.musimem.com.

Darrieussecq, Marie (2023), *Sleepless: A Memoir of Insomnia*, trans. Penny Hueston, London: Fitzcarraldo.

David, Angie (2013), *Sylvia Bataille*, Paris: Scheer.

David, Max (1973), 'Antologia critica', in *Saporetti*, Milan: Galleria Levi, npag.

De Crémone, L. (1927), 'Spectacles et concerts', *Figaro*, 16 January, p. 5.
Delaney, Frank (1996), 'Coffee without the Brandy', *The Observer*, 1 September, p. 4.
De Lardélec, Jean (1934), 'Paris-Soir', *Revue des lectures*, 3, 15 March, pp. 267–72.
Dukes, Gerry (2001), *Samuel Beckett*, London: Penguin.
Dumas, Alexandre (1843), *Filles, lorettes et courtisanes*, Paris: Dolin.
Dumesnil, Suzanne (1935a), *Musique Jeux: Pédagogie moderne – Premiers contacts de l'enfant et de la musique*, Paris: H. Lemoine.
Dumesnil, Suzanne (1935b), 'L'Amant de coeur', *Paris-Soir*, 30 June, p. 2.
Duthuit, Georges (1949), 'Notes about Contributors', *Transition Forty-Eight*, 4, pp. 151–5.
Echenoz, Jean (2001), *Jérôme Lindon*, Paris: Minuit.
Ellmann, Richard (1978), 'The Life of Sim Botchit', *New York Review of Books*, 15 June, pp. 3–8.
Fandos, Manolo (2024), 'Fandos-Beckett Relationship', trans. Julio Trujillo, personal collection.
Fernández, José Franscisco (2015), '"Minister of Horses": Samuel Beckett According to Fernando Arrabal', *Journal of Beckett Studies*, 24:2, pp. 223–41.
Fernández, José Francisco (2025), '*Le Petit Sot* Poems: Exploring the German Connection', *Samuel Beckett Today/Aujourd'hui* 37:1, pp. 23–37.
Fletcher, John (2016), 'My Conversations with Samuel Beckett', *Samuel Beckett Today/Aujourd'hui*, 28:1, pp. 29–34.
Fourcade, J.-F. (2016), *Autographes et manuscrits*, Paris: Fourcade.
Front Matter (1949), *Kenyon Review*, 11:3, npag.
Gallica (2000–24), Bibliothèque Nationale de France, https://gallica.bnf.fr/.
Gawann (1936), 'L'Edition musicale', *L'Art musical*, 26 June, p. 8.
Geelhaar, Christian (1973), *Paul Klee and the Bauhaus*, Bath: Adams & Dart.
Gibson, Andrew (2010), *Samuel Beckett*, London: Reaktion.
Gordon, Lois (1996), *The World of Samuel Beckett, 1906–1946*, New Haven, CT: Yale University Press.
Guggenheim, Peggy (1980), *Out of This Century: Confessions of an Art Addict*, London: Deutsch.
Gussow, Mel (1996), *Conversations with (and About) Beckett*, New York: Grove.
Harmon, Maurice, ed. (1998), *No Author Better Served: The Correspondence of Samuel Beckett and Alan Schneider*, Cambridge, MA: Harvard University Press.
Harvey, Lawrence E. (1970), *Samuel Beckett: Poet and Critic*, Princeton, NJ: Princeton University Press.

Hebert, Hugh (1980), 'Brief Encounter with a Stage Irishman', *The Guardian*, 17 May, p. 11.
Henri, Ch. and Etienne Singla (1869), 'J'aurai seize ans', Paris: Tessier.
Horovitz, Israel (1997), 'A Remembrance of Samuel Beckett', *Paris Review*, 142, pp. 189–93.
Huston, Nancy (2004), *Professeurs de désespoir*, Arles: Actes Sud.
Hutchings, William (1997), 'Review of *Damned to Fame: The Life of Samuel Beckett* by James Knowlson', *World Literature Today*, 71:3, pp. 597–8.
Insee [French National Institute of Statistics and Economic Studies] (2019–25), *Fichier des personnes décédées*, https://deces.matchid.io/search.
Israel, Calvin (1979), 'Review of *Samuel Beckett: A Biography* by Deirdre Bair', *Journal of Beckett Studies*, 4, pp. 80–5.
Jacometti, Nesto (1934), *Têtes de Montparnasse*, Paris: Villain.
Janvier, Ludovic (1969), *Samuel Beckett par lui-même*, Paris: Seuil.
Jonic, Bettina (2010), 'A Bizarre Lady', *London Magazine*, https://thelondonmagazine.org/article/with-and-without-sam/.
Juliet, Charles (1999), *Rencontres avec Samuel Beckett*, Paris: P.O.L.
Karagheuz, Hermine ([2002] 2021), *Roger Blin: Une dette d'amour*, Paris: Ypsilon.
Kędzierski, Marek (2011), 'Barbara Bray: In Her Own Words', *Modernism/modernity*, 18:4, pp. 887–97.
Knowlson, James (1996), *Damned to Fame: The Life of Samuel Beckett*, London: Bloomsbury.
Knowlson, James and John Haynes (2003), *Images of Beckett*, Cambridge: Cambridge University Press.
Knowlson, James and Elizabeth Knowlson, eds (2006), *Beckett Remembering/Remembering Beckett*, New York: Arcade.
Labreure, David (2000), *Louis-Ferdinand Céline, une pensée médicale*, Paris: Publibook.
Lamont, Rosette C. (1995), 'Beckett's Lost Play', *Theater Week*, 9:2, pp. 32–6.
Léger, Nathalie (2006), *Les vies silencieuses de Samuel Beckett*, Paris: Allia.
Levy, Jay A. (1998), 'Conversations with Samuel Beckett', in Cathleen Culotta Andonian (ed.), *The Critical Response to Samuel Beckett*, Westport, CT: Greenwood, pp. 195–206.
Lindon, Jérôme and Alfred Simon (1992), 'Avis', *Esprit*, 183:7, pp. 176–7.
Lindon, Mathieu (2023), *Une archive*, Paris: P.O.L.
Lucas, Hippolyte (1893), *Chants de divers pays (poésies inédites)*, Nantes: Société des Bibliophiles Bretons et de l'Histoire de Bretagne.
Maitron, Jean et al. (2007–24), *Le Maitron: Dictionnaire biographique, mouvement ouvrier, mouvement social*, https://maitron.fr/.

Martelli, H. (1936), 'Dumesnil (Suzanne), Pédagogie moderne', *Revue Musicale*, 168, p. 288.

Mélèse, Pierre (1966), *Beckett*, Paris: Seghers.

Memmi, Albert (1985), *Portrait du colonisé précédé du Portrait du colonisateur*, Paris: Gallimard.

Montague, John (2001), *Company: A Chosen Life*, London: Duckworth.

Moorjani, Angela (1978), 'Review of *Samuel Beckett: A Biography* by Deirdre Bair', *MLN*, 93:5, pp. 1106–15.

Morin, Emilie (2017), *Beckett's Political Imagination*, Cambridge: Cambridge University Press.

Nugent, Georgina, ed. (2023a), *Beckett's Women Contemporaries*, special issue of *Journal of Beckett Studies*, 32:1.

Nugent, Georgina (2023b), 'Unfathered Connections: Samuel Beckett and Djuna Barnes', *Journal of Beckett Studies*, 32:1, pp. 45–63.

O'Brien, John (2016), 'On Meeting Samuel Beckett', *Samuel Beckett Today/Aujourd'hui*, 28:1, pp. 56–62.

Olivier, Philippe (2002), 'Introduction', in *Musique: Ecole Normale de Musique de Paris Alfred Cortot*, Paris: Plume, pp. 111–24.

Overbeck, Lois More et al. (2024), *Chercher: Index to Samuel Beckett's Letters*, https://chercherbeckettletters.emory.edu/.

Pattie, David (2000), *The Complete Critical Guide to Samuel Beckett*, London: Routledge.

Pilling, John (2015), '"Dead before Morning": How Beckett's "Petit Sot" Never Got Properly Born', *Journal of Beckett Studies*, 24:2, pp. 198–209.

Renaud, Madeleine (2000), *La Déclaration d'amour*, Monaco: Editions du Rocher.

Renouard, Madeleine (1993), *Robert Pinget à la lettre: Entretiens avec Madeleine Renouard*, Paris: Belfond.

Robbe-Grillet, Catherine (2004), *Jeune mariée: Journal, 1957–1962*, Paris: Fayard.

Rosset, Barney (2009), 'Remembering Samuel Beckett', *Conjunctions*, 53, pp. 8–34.

Rosset, Barney (2016), *Rosset: My Life in Publishing and How I Fought Censorship*, New York: OR Books.

Royer, Corinne (2019), *Ce qui nous revient*, Arles: Actes Sud.

Ruffel, David (2013), 'Pinget Queer', *Romanic Review*, 104:2, pp. 127–45.

*Samuel Beckett: Silence to Silence*, film, directed by Seán O'Mórdha. Dublin: RTE, 1984.

Sardin, Pascale (2024a), 'On Writing a Translator's Biography: Bringing Barbara Bray out of the Archives', *Journal of Beckett Studies*, 33:2, pp. 181–200.

Sardin, Pascale (2024b), *Barbara Bray, A Woman of Letters: Translator, Radio Producer, Scriptwriter, Critic, and Theatre Director*, New York: Routledge.

Scharwath, Günter (1999), *Miniaturen zur Kunst- und Kulturgeschichte der Saarregion*, Saarbrücken: Die Mitte.

Scharwath, Günter (2017), *Das große Künstlerlexikon der Saar-Region*, Saarbrücken: Geistkirch.

Schneiderman, Leo (1988), *The Literary Mind: Portraits in Pain and Creativity*, New York: Insight.

Seaver, Richard (2011), *The Tender Hour of Twilight: Paris in the '50s, New York in the '60s: A Memoir of Publishing's Golden Age*, ed. Jeannette Seaver, New York: Farrar, Straus & Giroux.

Shainberg, Lawrence ([1987] 1992), 'Exorcising Beckett', in George Plimpton (ed.), *Writers at Work: The Paris Review Interviews*, 9th series, Harmondsworth: Penguin, pp. 1–35.

Simpson, Hannah (2018), 'Samuel Beckett and the Nobel Catastrophe', *Samuel Beckett Today/Aujourd'hui*, 30:2, pp. 337–52.

Stern, Anne (n.d.), 'Biographie de Paul Stern', *Convoi 77*, https://convoi77.org/deporte_bio/stern-paul/.

Stern, Richard (1991), 'Samuel Beckett', *Salmagundi*, 90–1, pp. 179–90.

Strathern, Paul (2005), *Beckett in 90 Minutes*, Chicago, IL: Dee.

Taylor, Karen (1988), *Alfred Cortot: His Interpretive Art and Teachings*, dissertation, Indiana University.

Tholozan, Jean-Pierre (n.d.), Déchevaux-Dumesnil family tree, Geneanet, https://gw.geneanet.org/.

Tholozan-Warluzel, Michèle (2024), 'Suzanne: Fragments of Memories', trans. Emilie Morin, *Journal of Beckett Studies*, 33:2, pp. 137–61.

Timbrell, Charles (1999), *French Pianism: A Historical Perspective*, 2nd ed., Portland, OR: Amadeus.

Van Hulle, Dirk and Pim Verhulst (2017), 'Notes on a Newly Discovered Draft of the Poem "Le Petit Sot"', *Journal of Beckett Studies*, 26:2, pp. 206–20.

Van Hulle, Dirk, Mark Nixon and Vincent Neyt, eds. (2016), *The Beckett Digital Library: A Digital Genetic Edition*, Beckett Digital Manuscript Project, Brussels: ASP/University Press Antwerp, www.beckettarchive.org.

Van Velde, Bram (2012), *Lettres à Marthe Arnaud, Jacques Putman, Françoise Porte*, ed. Gilles Béraud, Martin Lacroix and Françoise Porte, Lagrasse: Verdier.

Vignes, Henri, Jean-Etienne Huret and Les Libraires Associés, eds. (2011), *NRF Gallimard, 100 ans d'édition*, Paris: Librairie Vignes.

Vines, Alan (1962), 'Artist with a Camera', *British Journal of Photography*, 109:5304, p. 200.

*Waiting for Beckett*, film, directed by John Reilly and Melissa Shaw Smith. New York: Global Village, 1993.

Walker, Tim (2014), 'Mandrake', *Daily Telegraph*, 30 April, p. 6.

Wheatley, David (2002), 'Labours Unfinished', *Irish Times*, 27 April, p. 11.

Whelan, Robert (1985), *Robert Capa: A Biography*, Lincoln: University of Nebraska Press.

Whitelaw, Billie (1995), *Billie Whitelaw ... Who He?*, London: Hodder & Stoughton.

Wick, Rainer (2000), *Teaching at the Bauhaus*, Oggebio: Hatje Cantz.

Williams, Val (1989), *Ida Kar: Photographer, 1908–1974*, London: Virago.

# Acknowledgements

Sincerest thanks to Michèle Tholozan-Warluzel, who entrusted me with her memories and offered to show me her family papers before I knew that doing this work was possible and that I would do it; to Anne-Marie Colombard, who brought Suzanne to life with a generosity for which I am deeply grateful; to Claude Salzman, who talked about his family with the same generosity; to Manolo Fandos and the late Marthe Gautier, for sharing their memories; to Alexandre Dandelot, for sharing his research on his family. Warm thanks also to Jean-Pierre Tholozan, Zoubeida Salzman, José Antonio Arias, Rea Coskinas Saporetti and Julio Trujillo; to my wonderful family; to the many archivists who facilitated my research; to the Series Editors, Mark Nixon and Dirk Van Hulle, the external readers, Ray Ryan and the CUP Elements production team; to the University of York's F. R. Leavis Fund and my York colleagues, especially Boriana Alexandrova, Jennie Batchelor, John Bowen, Sophie Coulombeau and Helen Smith; and all those, further away, too numerous to name, who responded gracefully and with interest to my research.

Cambridge Elements =

# Beckett Studies

Dirk Van Hulle
*University of Oxford*
Dirk Van Hulle is Professor of Bibliography and Modern Book History at the University of Oxford and director of the Centre for Manuscript Genetics at the University of Antwerp.

Mark Nixon
*University of Reading*
Mark Nixon is Professor of Modern Literature and Beckett Studies at the University of Reading and the Co-Director of the Beckett International Foundation.

**About the Series**

This series presents cutting-edge research by distinguished and emerging scholars, providing space for the most relevant debates informing Beckett studies as well as neglected aspects of his work. In times of technological development, religious radicalism, unprecedented migration, gender fluidity, environmental and social crisis, Beckett's works find increased resonance. Cambridge Elements in Beckett Studies is a key resource for readers interested in the current state of the field.

# Cambridge Elements

# Beckett Studies

## Elements in the Series

*Beckett and Sade*
Jean-Michel Rabaté

*Beckett's Intermedial Ecosystems: Closed Space Environments across the Stage, Prose and Media Works*
Anna McMullan

*Samuel Beckett and Cultural Nationalism*
Shane Weller

*Absorption and Theatricality: On* Ghost Trio
Conor Carville

*Carnivals of Ruin: Beckett, Ireland, and the Festival Form*
Trish McTighe

*Beckett and Stein*
Georgina Nugent

*Insufferable: Beckett, Gender and Sexuality*
Daniela Caselli

*Bad Godots: 'Vladimir Emerges from the Barrel' and Other Interventions*
S. E. Gontarski

*Beckett and Cioran*
Steven Matthews

*Beckett and Derrida*
James Martell

*Pilgrim's Gress: The Beckett Walk*
Andre Furlani

*Suzanne Dumesnil, Suzanne Beckett*
Emilie Morin

A full series listing is available at: www.cambridge.org/eibs

For EU product safety concerns, contact us at Calle de José Abascal, 56–1°,
28003 Madrid, Spain or eugpsr@cambridge.org.

www.ingramcontent.com/pod-product-compliance
Lightning Source LLC
Chambersburg PA
CBHW071817071025
33697CB00027B/550